Duplex and Townhome Plans

 **Designs for Multi-Family Living**

Design 7458, page 34

- ◆ Multi-Family Designs 3
- ◆ Backyard Playsets 54
- ◆ How to Order Blueprints 56

Published by Home Planners, LLC
Wholly owned by Hanley-Wood, Inc.

Editorial and Corporate Offices:
3275 West Ina Road, Suite 110
Tucson, Arizona 85741

Distribution Center:
29333 Lorie Lane
Wixom, Michigan 48393

Rickard D. Bailey, CEO and Publisher
Stephen Williams, Director of Sales & Marketing
Cindy Coatsworth Lewis, Director of Publishing
Jan Prideaux, Senior Editor
Marian E. Haggard, Editor
Sara Lisa Rappaport, Manufacturing Coordinator
Matthew S. Kauffman, Graphic Designer

First Printing: January 1999

10 9 8 7 6 5 4 3 2 1

All floor plans and elevations copyright by the individual designers and may not be reproduced by any means without written permission. All text, design and illustrative material copyright ©1999 by Home Planners, LLC, wholly owned by Hanley-Wood, Inc., Tucson, Arizona 85741. All rights reserved. No part of this publication may be reproduced in any form or by any means—electronic, mechanical, photomechanical, recorded or otherwise—without the prior written permission of the publisher.

Printed in the United States of America

ISBN: 1-881955-59-1

Design Q453, page 29

Design 7452

Square Footage Unit A: 1,115
Square Footage Unit B: 1,052

◆ The only big difference between these two attractive units is the garage. Unit A has a two-car garage to complement its interior, while Unit B has a one-car garage. Both units feature a spacious living room with a fireplace and a box-bay window. The angled kitchen offers a peninsula with a sink, and provides easy service to the dining room. Here, a patio awaits to accommodate dining alfresco. The master bedroom suite is complete with a walk-in closet and a private bath. The den—or make it a second bedroom—has access to a large linen closet as well as a full hall bath.

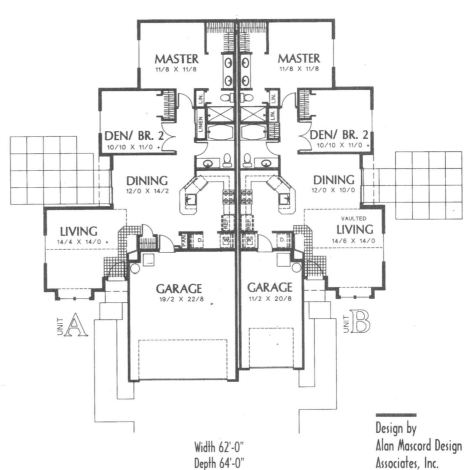

Width 62'-0"
Depth 64'-0"

Design by
Alan Mascord Design
Associates, Inc.

Design U192

Square Footage: 1,300 per unit

◆ This attractive duplex is perfectly designed for the family just starting out, or for empty nesters who need less room now that the kids have grown and gone. The units mirror one another and have many amenities to offer. A spacious living area encompasses both the living room as well as a dining area, and is conveniently located to the efficient kitchen. A wooden deck is just outside the breakfast nook, providing a place for dining alfresco. The master bedroom is complete with a dual-bowl lavatory and a walk-in closet. The front bedroom—or make it a cozy study—has a full bath and two linen closets available to it.

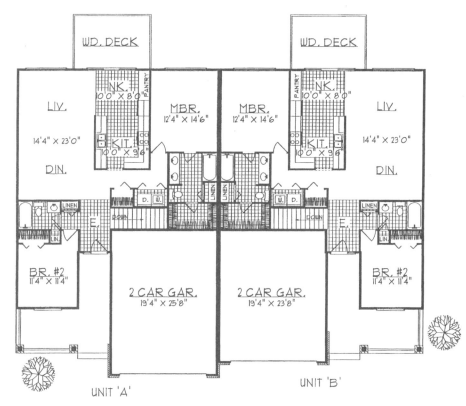

Width 76'-0"
Depth 55'-0"

Design by
Ahmann Design, Inc.

Design Z047

Square Footage: 834 per unit

◆ Two gables adorn the front of this fine duplex, while inside, matching units offer a place to call home. The foyer opens directly into the living area where there is space for both a living room and a dining area. The kitchen is

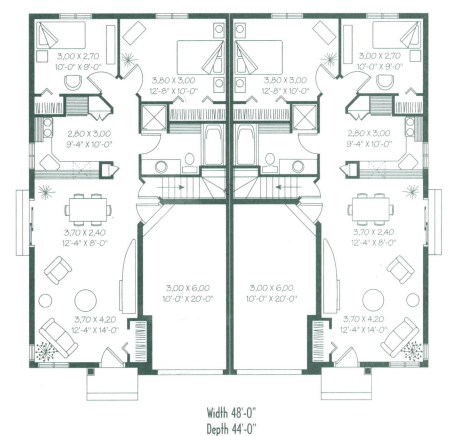

Design by
Drummond Designs, Inc.

Width 48'-0"
Depth 44'-0"

Design C503

Square Footage: 856 per unit

◆ Perfect for couples just starting out, or for those who don't need the space of a large house anymore, this gabled and sided duplex will be the envy of its neighbors. A side entry which opens into the living room is just the beginning for these matching units. A U-shaped kitchen offers a corner sink with a bright window, and a pass-through to the dining area nearby. Two bedrooms, one a master bedroom with a large walk-in closet, share a full hall bath. The one-car garage features plenty of storage space, for lawn equipment or bikes.

Design by
Piercy & Barclay
Designers, Inc.

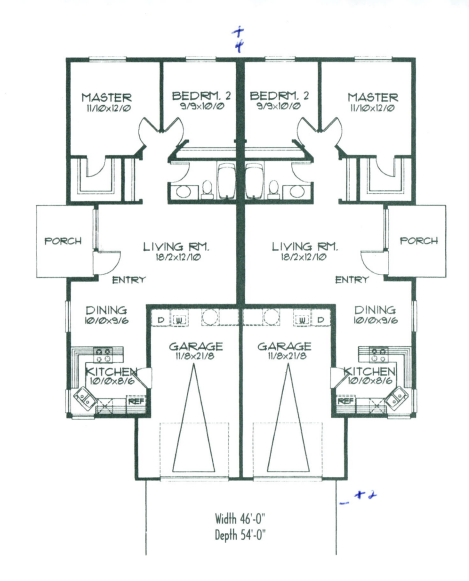

Width 46'-0"
Depth 54'-0"

DESIGN C512

Square Footage: 1,226 per unit

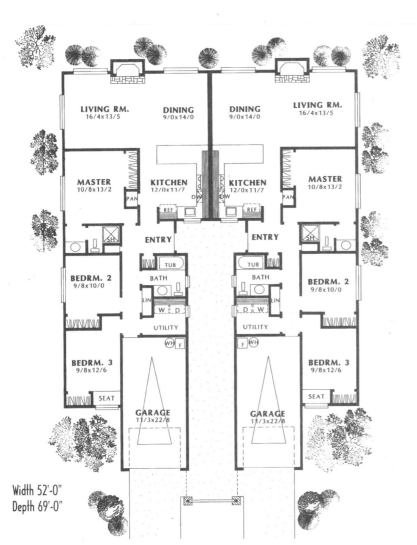

Width 52'-0"
Depth 69'-0"

◆ A covered walkway to the front door is just one of the many charms of this fine duplex. Each unit offers the same amenities, ranging from the spacious living/dining room area warmed by a fireplace, the U-shaped kitchen and three bedrooms, to two full baths and a utility room. The front bedroom offers a built-in window seat, while the master bedroom is enhanced by a private full bath. Storage is evident with a pantry in the kitchen, a closet by the front door and a large linen closet in the hall. A one-car garage is available to keep the rain off when parking the car.

Design by
Piercy & Barclay
Designers, Inc.

Design C505

Square Footage: 937 per unit

◆ With contemporary lines, this fine duplex will look good in any neighborhood. Mirror images of each other, the amenities abound in these two-bedroom units. A fireplace warms the living room, with a nearby dining area offering access through sliding glass doors to a side patio. The U-shaped kitchen features a pantry and plenty of counter and cabinet space. Two bedrooms reside at the rear of the home, and share a full hall bath. Note the convenience of the washer and dryer area. The one-car garage works well to separate the living areas of both units.

Design by
Piercy & Barclay
Designers, Inc.

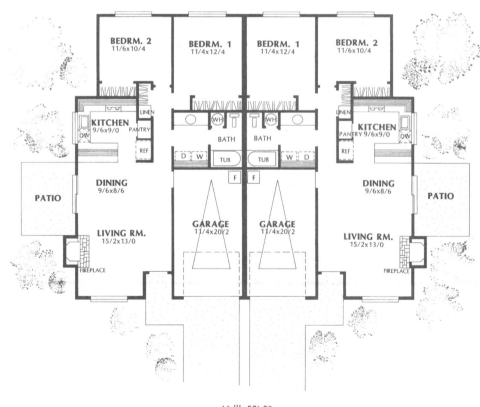

Width 59'-0"
Depth 45'-0"

Design 7451

Square Footage: 1,367 per unit

◆ With the two-car garages facing different directions, this duplex might easily pass for a single family unit at first glance. The rest of their layouts are identical, however, with many amenities. The master suite is large and comfortable, offering a walk-in closet and a private bath. There is a formal area for entertaining, with the living room featuring a vaulted ceiling and a bay window. A family room is available to relax in—complete with a fireplace. The large kitchen is easily accessible to both the dining room and the family room, providing serving ease.

Design by
Alan Mascord Design
Associates, Inc.

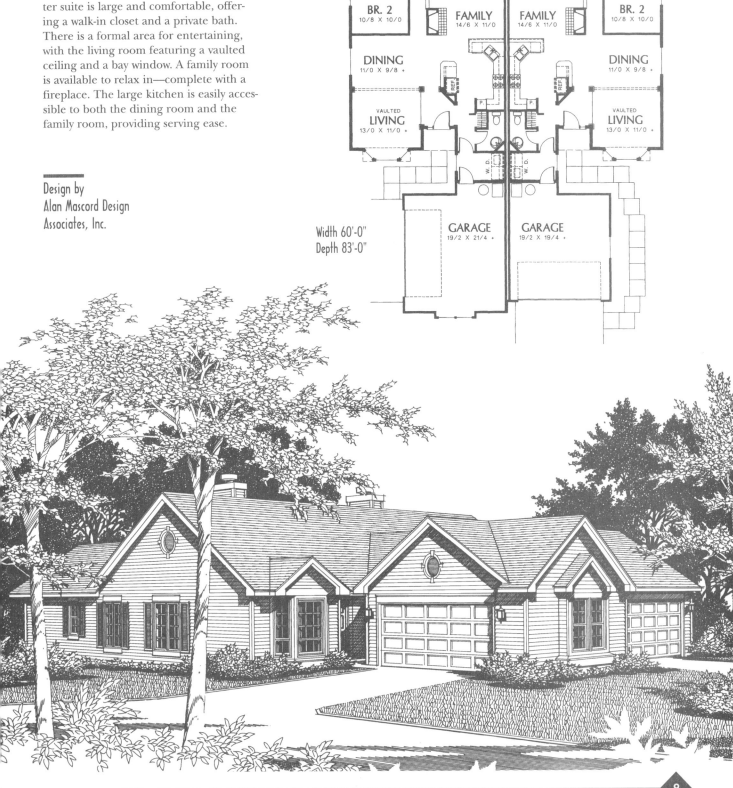

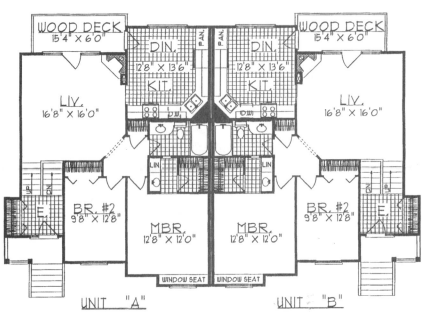

Design by Ahmann Design, Inc.

UNIT "A"   UNIT "B"

Design U188

Main Level: 1,050 square feet
Lower Level: 528 square feet
Total: 1,578 square feet per unit

◆ When Bob and Mark found out that they were both getting transferred to the new headquarters, they decided to look for homes near each other. Their families had been friends since Bob asked Mark to be in his wedding, and both men had sons on the same little league team. After a bit of futile searching, Bob stumbled across an attractive development of duplex homes. Their thought was that their families could rely on each other and be safe when the company sent the men off on business trips. The units offered two bedrooms, an eat-in kitchen, a fireplace in the living room and a deck for star gazing—all on the main level, while a third bedroom, a full bath and a good-size recreation room completed the lower level. Both units offered a two-car garage. The combination of a cozy place to live and the close proximity of friends was too much for either of them to let pass by.

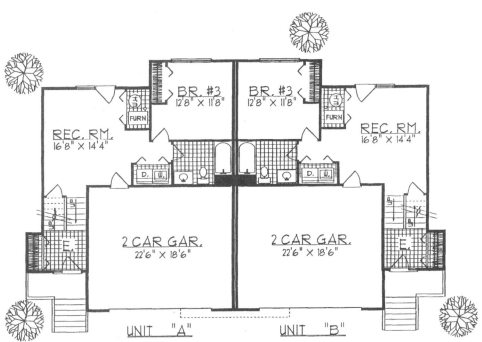

Width 66'-0"
Depth 39'-6"

Design C508

Square Footage: 1,032 per unit

◆ Perfect for an empty nester, or a couple just starting out, this set of units offer many amenities. Mirror images of each other, the spacious units both open from the side directly into the living room. Here, a fireplace waits to warm cool fall evenings. A dining room has easy access to the U-shaped kitchen and provides plenty of natural light from its many windows. Two spacious bedrooms share a full hall bath, with the convenience of a washer and dryer right there. The one-car garage will easily shelter the family vehicle.

Design by
Piercy & Barclay
Designers, Inc.

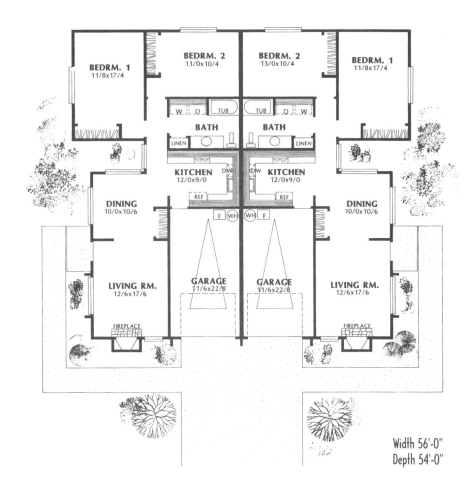

Width 56'-0"
Depth 54'-0"

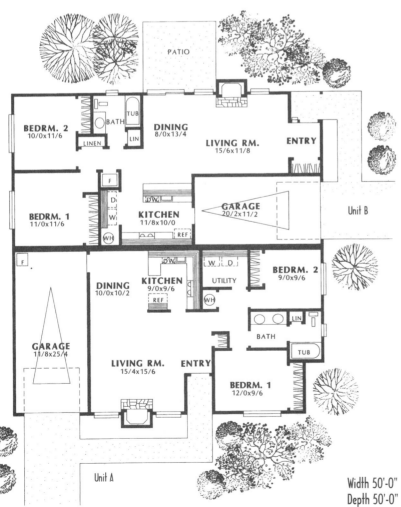

Width 50'-0"
Depth 50'-0"

Design C506

Square Footage: 915 unit A/960 unit B

◆ Set up for a corner lot, this fine duplex home will blend into any neighborhood. Offering the same amenities in slightly different configurations, these units would be good for people building their first home or for those who don't need much space anymore. Each unit offers a comfortable living room with a fireplace, a dining area convenient to the efficient kitchen and two bedrooms sharing a full bath. A one-car garage will surely shelter the family car. Note how unit B offers a dining patio while unit A has a separate utility room for the washer and dryer.

Design by
Piercy & Barclay
Designers, Inc.

DESIGN C507

Square Footage: 951 per unit

◆ Bring the outdoors in with these fine duplex units. An atrium is designed right in the middle of each plan, to help flood the area with natural light. The C-shaped kitchens offer pantries and a serving counter into the dining room. The large living rooms are near the two bedrooms, and a full hall bath—with a window into the atrium—is near by. Access to the atrium is near the living room.

Design by
Piercy & Barclay
Designers, Inc.

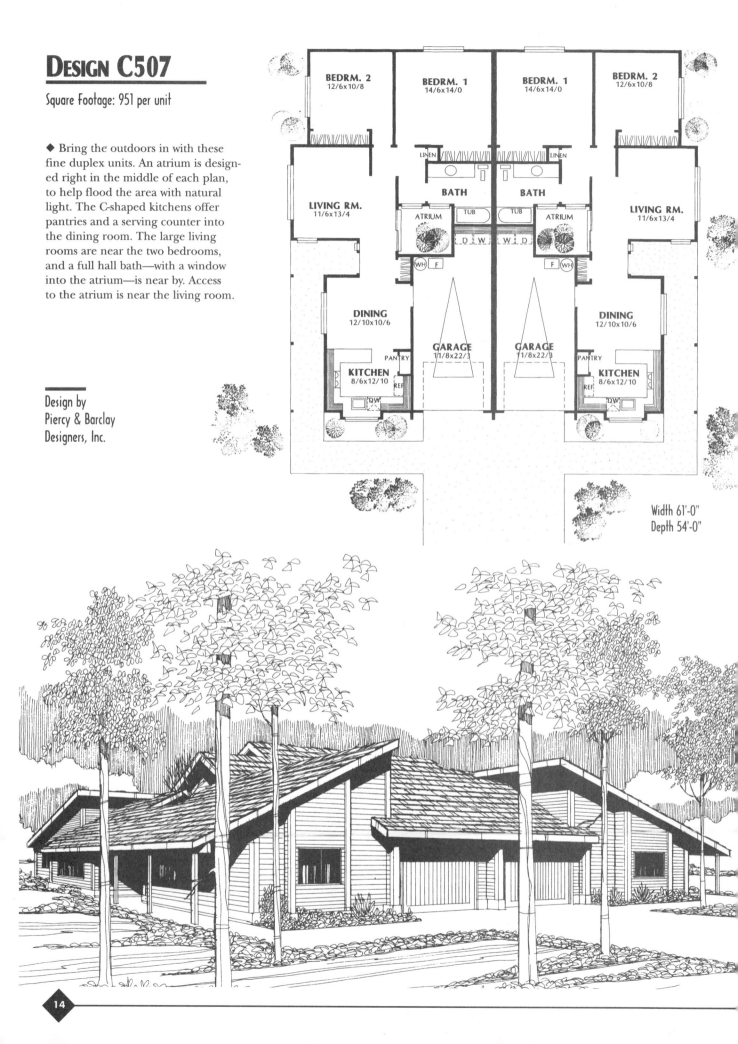

Design C513

Square Footage: 1,074 unit A/1,318 unit B

◆ Whether you need two or three bedrooms, this fine duplex will be a delight to call home. Unit A offers such amenities as a sunken living room complete with a warming fireplace and access to the rear patio through sliding glass doors, two closets and a private dressing room in Bedroom 1, a large linen closet and an efficient U-shaped kitchen. A one-car garage completes this unit. Unit B presents a combined dining/family room with access to a private patio, a large living room with a fireplace and three bedrooms—one a master suite with a walk-in closet and a private bath. The two-car garage will easily shelter the family fleet.

Design by
Piercy & Barclay
Designers, Inc.

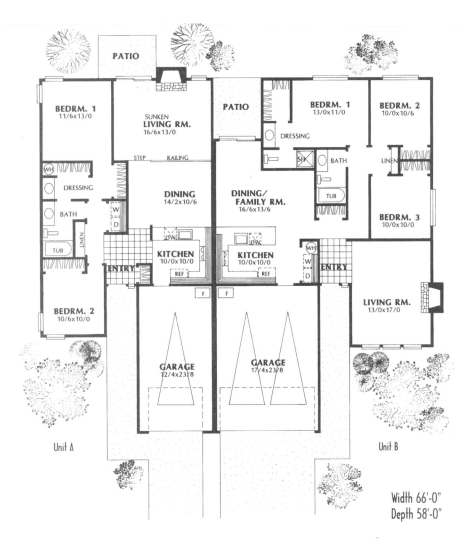

Width 66'-0"
Depth 58'-0"

Design C509

Square Footage: 1,175 unit A/1,120 unit B

◆ Looking more like a single family home, this duplex has plenty to offer. Unit A consists of a delightful U-shaped kitchen with easy access to the dining area. A large living room features a warming fireplace flanked by windows. Bedroom 1 offers a spacious walk-in wardrobe and shares a full hall bath with Bedroom 2. In unit B, similar amenities wait, with the addition of sliding glass doors to a patio in the dining area, and a separate area for the washer and dryer. Two one-car garages are available for sheltering the family vehicles.

Design by
Piercy & Barclay
Designers, Inc.

Width 64'-0"
Depth 50'-0"

Design C510

Square Footage: 1,170 per unit

◆ Mirror images of each other and filled with amenities, these two units will be pure heaven to live in. The vaulted great room, complete with a fireplace, and the adjacent dining room with access to the rear patio, are just two of these tempting bonuses. The efficient kitchen offers a corner sink with windows and an angled peninsula to make serving a breeze. A master suite features access to a private patio, a walk-in closet and a private bath. Bedroom 2 has its own hall bath, and access to the front covered courtyard.

Design by
Piercy & Barclay
Designers, Inc.

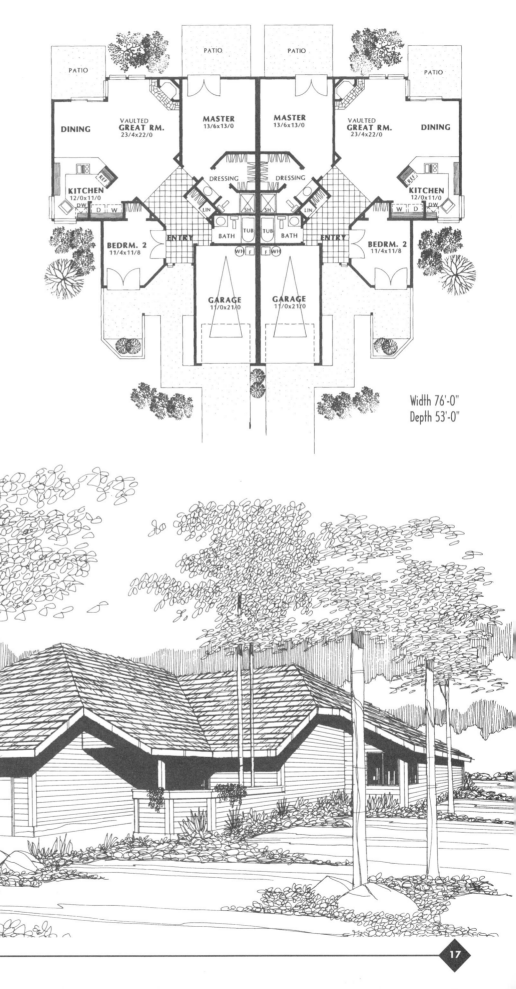

Width 76'-0"
Depth 53'-0"

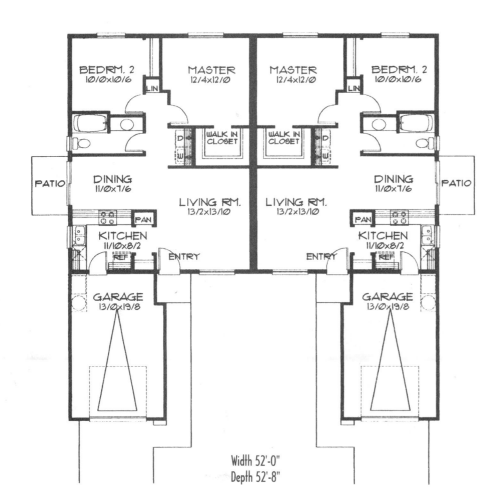

Width 52'-0"
Depth 52'-8"

Design C502

Square Footage: 850 per unit

◆ Petite yet sweet, this two-bedroom duplex is perfect for empty-nesters or couples just starting out. The entry opens directly into the living room, with the efficient kitchen to the right. A dining area is enhanced by access to a small patio. Note the pass-through from the kitchen to this area, making serving a breeze. The sleeping zone is located to the rear of the home and includes a master suite with a walk-in closet, and another bedroom, both sharing a hall bath. A one-car garage will help shelter the family vehicle.

Design by
Piercy & Barclay
Designers, Inc.

Design C514

Square Footage: 1,298 per unit

◆ A covered walkway guides you to the vaulted front entry, which leads to the various living areas of this fine duplex. The living room features a warming fireplace flanked by windows, while the adjacent dining area has access to the rear patio. The kitchen offers plenty of counter and cabinet space and also offers easy access to both the dining area and the living room. An attached nook serves casual meal times with ease. Two secondary bedrooms share a hall bath while the master suite offers two closets and a private bath. A two-car garage is available for the family fleet and offers plenty of storage.

Design by
Piercy & Barclay
Designers, Inc.

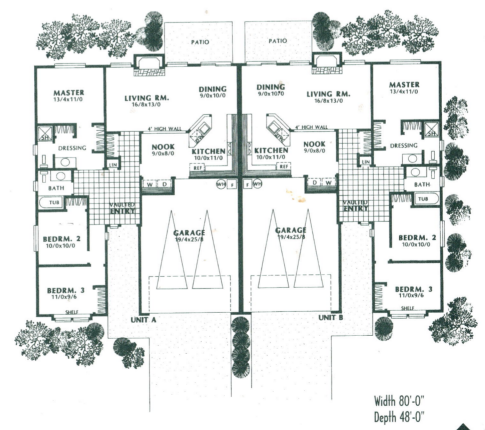

Width 80'-0"
Depth 48'-0"

DESIGN C511

Square Footage: 1,178 per unit

◆ Full of amenities, this duplex is a delight to live in. With a kitchen filled with counter and cabinet space, a corner sink and an eating bar, the gourmet of the family will surely be pleased. Vaulted ceilings soar over the dining room as well as the living room, which features a warming fireplace and access to the rear patio. The front bedroom shares a tub and toilet with the master bedroom, but has its own lavatory. The master bedroom is sunken and vaulted and is enhanced by two closets and a separate dressing area.

Design by
Piercy & Barclay
Designers, Inc.

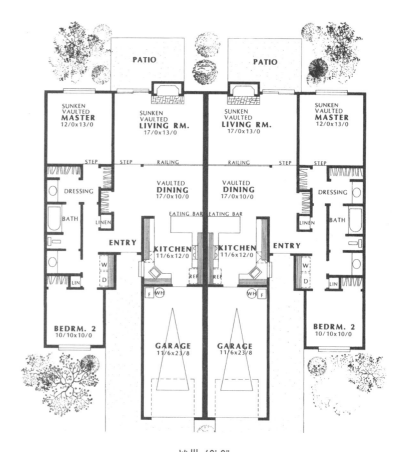

Width 60'-0"
Depth 60'-0"

DESIGN C517

First Floor: 696 square feet
Second Floor: 603 square feet
Total: 1,299 per unit square feet

◆ Two's run rampant over this fine duplex: two levels, two-car garages, two decks each, two secondary bedrooms. Other enhancing amenities include the entire first floor having vaulted ceilings, a fireplace in the great room, a dining deck for outdoor meals, plenty of storage and the sleeping zone located downstairs to offer privacy. The master bedroom is large and offers plenty of closet space. All three bedrooms share a full hall bath.

Design by
Piercy & Barclay
Designers, Inc.

Width 80'-0"
Depth 42'-0"

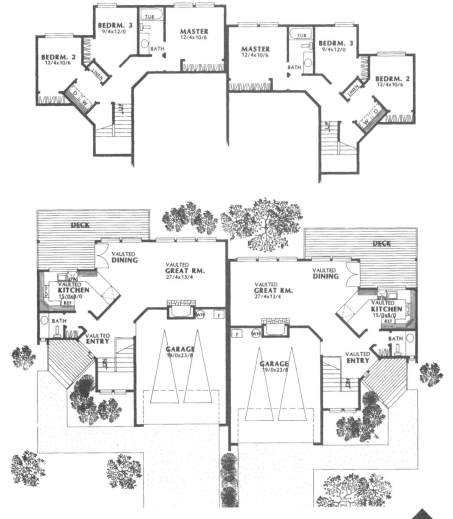

Design C519

First Floor: 750/950 square feet
Second Floor: 800/385 square feet
Total: 1,550/1,335 square feet

Width 68'-0"
Depth 48'-0"

◆ Variety is the spice of life they say, and this fine duplex is full of spice! Though both units have three bedrooms, they couldn't have more differences unless they were traditional single family use. Unit A starts with a large breakfast area, perfect for early morning gathers or your first cup of coffee. A corner kitchen has easy access to the vaulted morning room and the dining area. A fireplace waits to warm cool evenings in the great room. Upstairs, a lavish master suite features a walk-in closet and a private bath. Two other bedrooms—one a huge room, perfect for a games room—share a full hall bath. Unit B has many of the same amenities, with the main difference being layout. Here, the master suite is located on the main floor, providing privacy for both the homeowner and the kids.

Design by
Piercy & Barclay
Designers, Inc.

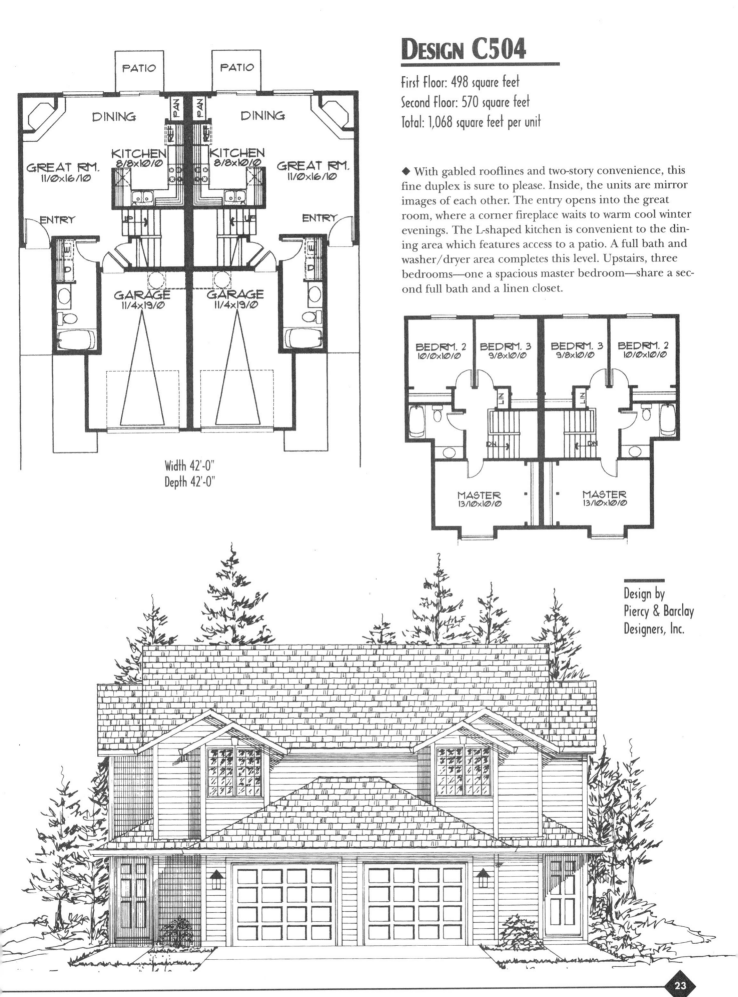

Design 7460

First Floor: 655 square feet
Second Floor: 809 square feet
Total: 1,464 square feet per unit

◆ Four gables, siding-and-brick facade and columns framing a covered porch all combine to give this fine duplex plenty of curb appeal. Inside, a two-story foyer leads to the great room, where a through-fireplace is shared with the efficient U-shaped kitchen. The nearby dining area offers access to the rear yard. Upstairs, two secondary bedrooms share a full bath with a dual-bowl vanity, while the master bedroom suite features a walk-in closet and a private bath. A laundry room finishes out this level. The two-car garage will easily shelter the family fleet.

Design by
Alan Mascord Design
Associates, Inc.

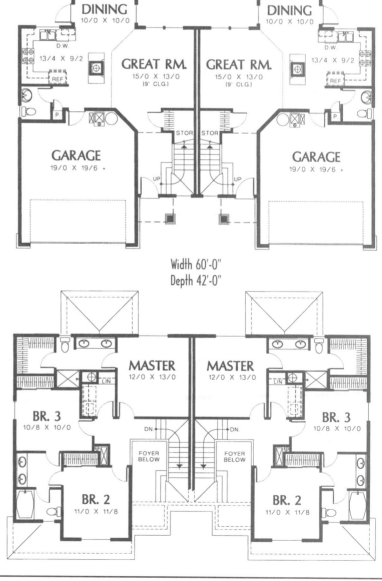

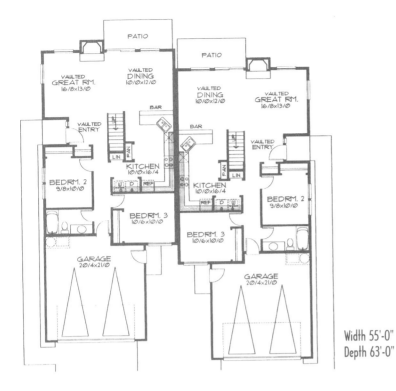

Width 55'-0"
Depth 63'-0"

Design C501

First Floor: 1,038 square feet
Second Floor: 564 square feet
Total: 1,602 square feet per unit

◆ With their entries on the side for each unit, privacy is assured in this fine duplex. The vaulted entry leads to the vaulted great room, where a warming fireplace waits to take the chill off cool winter evenings. This room flows nicely into the vaulted dining room, which is within easy serving distance of the efficient kitchen. Two bedrooms share a full bath and complete this level. upstairs, a vaulted loft with skylights is perfect for study, reading or a game area. Also on this level, the master bedroom suite is sure to please with a walk-in closet and a private bath.

Design by
Piercy & Barclay
Designers, Inc.

Design 7457

First Floor: 723/789 square feet
Second Floor: 711/708 square feet
Total: 1,434/1,496 square feet

Design by
Alan Mascord Design
Associates, Inc.

◆ Joseph had just gotten his first official job as an attorney, and decided that his old apartment wasn't up to the standard he was now aiming at, so he went house hunting. After looking at a number of single family homes, he realized he wasn't going to have the time and resources to care for an individual house quite yet, so with that in mind he focused on the expanding selection of duplexes going up on the west side of town. When he toured through the development, Joseph realized the builder had chosen to use a number of different stock plans to add variety to the neighborhood. And as he walked through a few of the houses, Joseph also noticed that the separate units of each duplex weren't an exact duplicate of each other. Not only were the facades a bit different, the layouts inside offered variety and individuality. For instance, the garages might open next to each other, but the front doors were on opposite corners of the home. The design that caught Joseph's eye, as well as his heart, was one that kept up the individual theme. The unit he decided to buy was a two-story, three-bedroom plan, with a two-car garage. The great room offered a warming fireplace, while the dining area had easy access to the L-shaped kitchen. The upstairs consisted of two family bedrooms sharing a hall bath, and a master suite with its own private bath.

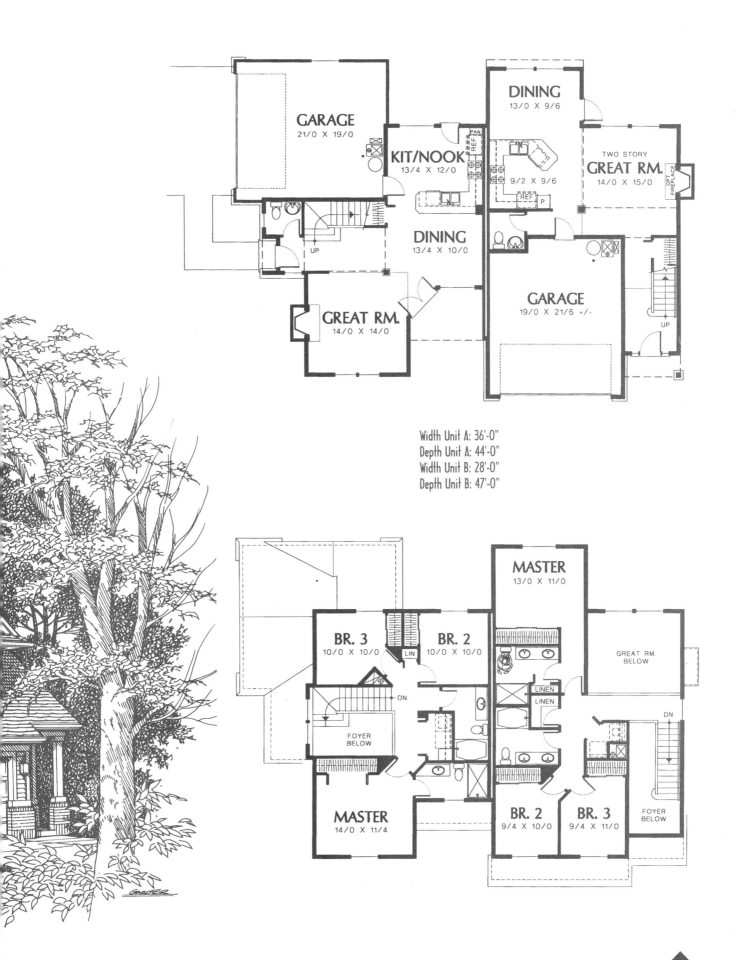

Design C500

First Floor: 1,004 square feet
Second Floor: 993 square feet
Total: 1,997 square feet

◆ Just a touch of variety with gables really dresses up this fine two-story duplex home. Inside, they are near mirror images of each other and offer the same amenities. Skylights brighten up the spacious great room, where a fireplace furthers the enhancement. The C-shaped kitchen features a pantry, tons of counter and cabinet space and a serving bar into the dining area. Here, sliding glass doors offer access to a rear patio. Upstairs, two family bedrooms share a full bath and access to a large storage closet. The master bedroom suite is designed to pamper, with a walk-in closet and a sumptuous private bath complete with a spa tub.

Width 56'-0"
Depth 60'-0"

Design by
Piercy & Barclay
Designers, Inc.

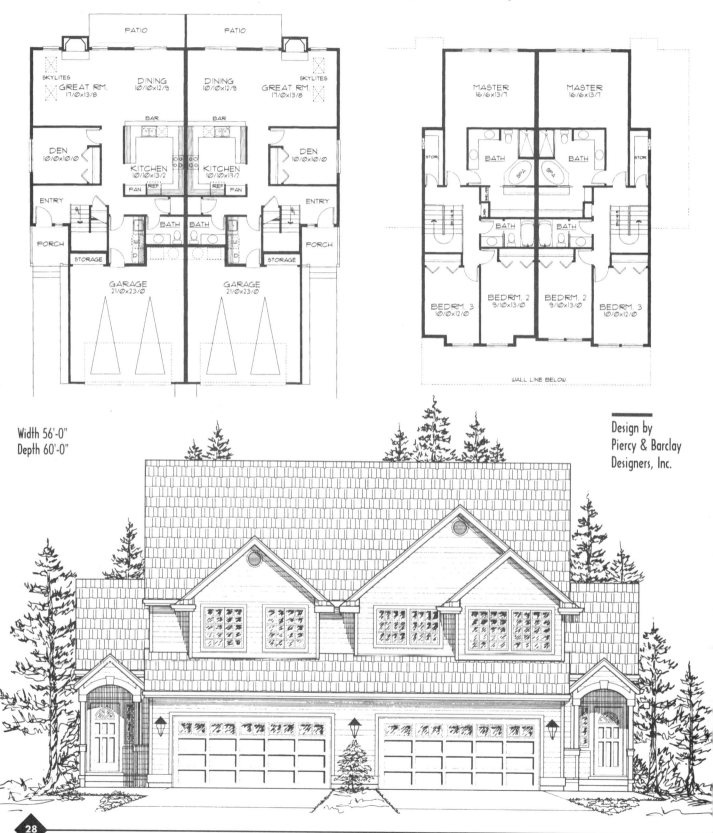

Design by
Select Home Designs

Design Q453

First Floor Unit: 1,453 square feet
Second Floor Unit: 1,438 square feet

◆ This economical two-story duplex provides great curb appeal and plenty of space. The first floor features a 1,453 square foot unit with three bedrooms, a U-shaped kitchen and two full baths. The dining/living room is warmed by a gas fireplace and boasts a half-wall overlooking the rear foyer. The second floor has a self-contained 1,438 square foot unit also with three bedrooms. Here, a living room with a gas fireplace is more separate from the dining area, where space is allowed for a buffet. The master bedrooms in both units are served by ample closets and private baths.

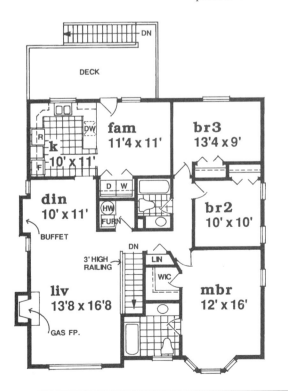

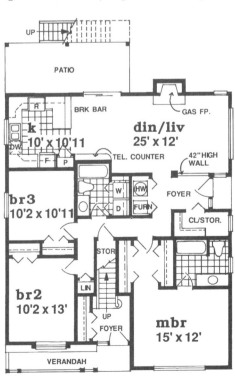

Width 36'-0"
Depth 43'-0"

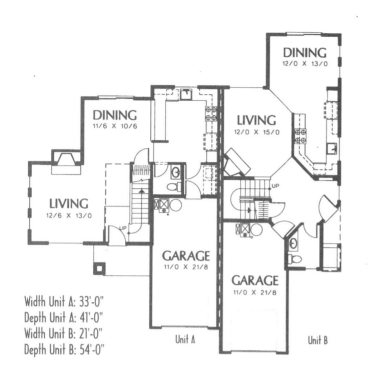

Width Unit A: 33'-0"
Depth Unit A: 41'-0"
Width Unit B: 21'-0"
Depth Unit B: 54'-0"

Unit A   Unit B

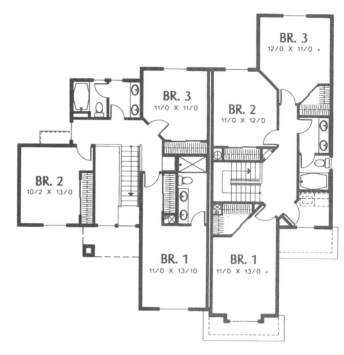

Design 7454

First Floor: 654/651 square feet
Second Floor: 817/812 square feet
Total: 1,471/1,463 square feet

Design by
Alan Mascord Design
Associates, Inc.

◆ Here is a beautiful two-story stock plan that looks like a large single-family home more than a duplex, and will blend in with any neighborhood. Each layout includes a U-shaped kitchen, a formal dining room, a living room with a fireplace and three bedrooms upstairs. Other amenities include sliding glass doors out to the rear yard, plenty of counter and cabinet space and two full baths upstairs.

Design 7455

First Floor: 596 square feet
Second Floor: 601 square feet
Total: 1,197 square feet

◆ Petite yet cozy, with a vaulted great room warmed by a fireplace, a U-shaped kitchen with lots of counter and cabinet space, and an upstairs sleeping zone, this two-story duplex will fit almost any lifestyle. Sliding glass doors lead from the great room to the rear yard. Upstairs, the two bedrooms share a full bath, with the front room featuring a vaulted ceiling. A cozy den finishes out this level, offering a perfect place for study, reading or a home office.

Design by
Alan Mascord Design
Associates, Inc.

Width 40'-0"
Depth 53'-0"

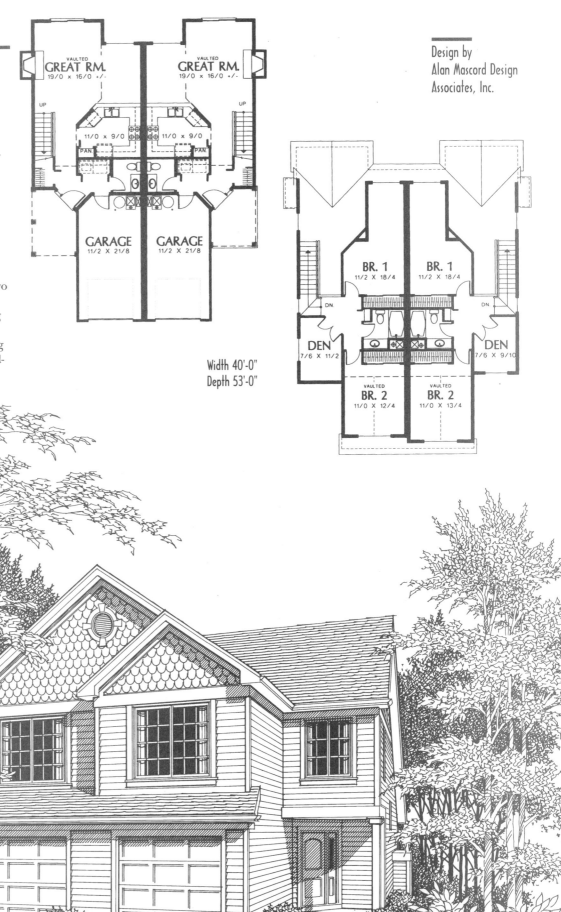

Design 7456

First Floor: 723/722 square feet
Second Floor: 710/681 square feet
Total: 1,433/1,403 square feet

◆ Two-story, three-bedroom homes that had the look of Colonial Americana, yet were up-to-date with many amenities—who could ask for more? Each unit includes a formal dining room, a spacious great room with a fireplace and a well-equipped kitchen on the main floor, with the sleeping zone located on the second floor. Here, a master bedroom suite offers a private bath, while two family bedrooms share a hall bath. Two-car garages are featured with each unit.

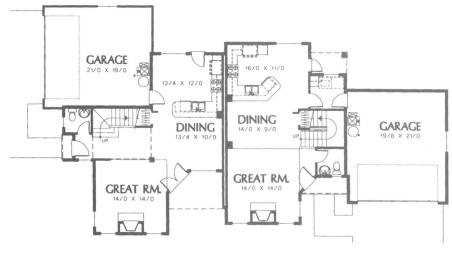

Width Unit A: 36'-0"
Depth Unit A: 44'-0"
Width Unit B: 44'-0"
Depth Unit B: 35'-0"

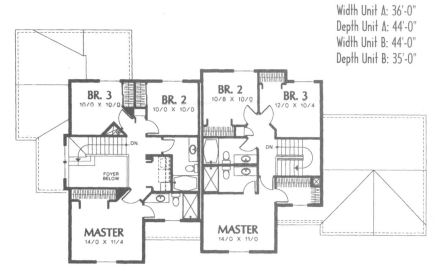

Design by
Alan Mascord Design
Associates, Inc.

Design C525

First Floor: 1,022 square feet
Second Floor: 509 square feet
Total: 1,531 square feet per unit

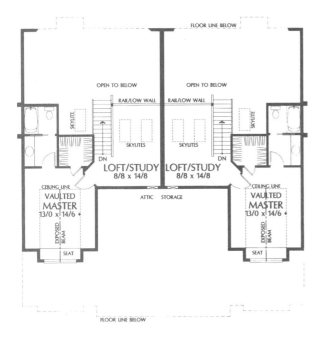

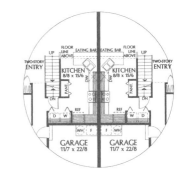

Width 52'-0"
Depth 52'-0"

◆ Gables, multi-paned windows and a touch of shingle-work combines to give this duplex a welcoming atmosphere. Side entries provide privacy, and usher you into a two-story foyer. Skylights above flood the area with natural light. The vaulted living and dining rooms work well together if you like to entertain. A fireplace and sliding glass doors in these rooms furthers the appeal. Two bedrooms share a full bath and make up the main-level sleeping zone. Upstairs, a vaulted master suite is designed to pamper with a walk-in closet and a private bath.

Design by
Piercy & Barclay
Designers, Inc.

Design by
Alan Mascord Design
Associates, Inc.

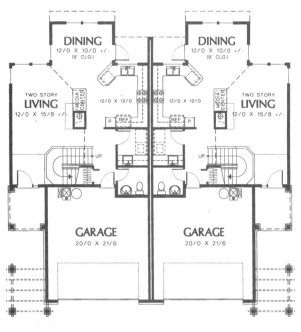

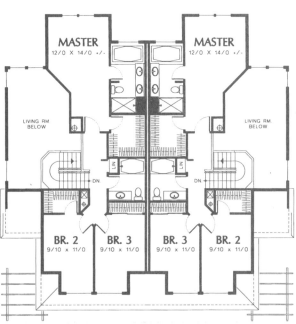

Width 56'-0"
Depth 56'-0"

Design 7458

First Floor: 785 square feet
Second Floor: 902 square feet
Total: 1,687 square feet

◆ With shingles and stone work, a trellis-covered front walk and twin gables, this fine two-story duplex is sure to please. Inside, the two-story living room greets friends and family alike, offering a fireplace and built-in media center for cozy get-togethers. The C-shaped kitchen features a window over the sink, plenty of counter and cabinet space and a serving counter into the dining room. A laundry room and a half bath complete this level. Upstairs, two secondary bedrooms—one with a walk-in closet—share a full hall bath. The master suite offers a large walk-in closet and a pampering private bath.

Design by
Piercy & Barclay
Designers, Inc.

Design C523

First Floor: 765 square feet
Second Floor: 765 square feet
Total: 1,530 square feet per unit

◆ The house of six gables? Well, you'd be off by one with this duplex, but you might fit more people into it! Two separate units, mirror images of each other and still roomy enough for a growing family. A covered porch leads to a vaulted entry which opens into the vaulted living room. Here, a fireplace waits to warm cool winter evenings.

The L-shaped kitchen offers an eating bar and easy access to the dining area. A patio is just beyond the dining room, providing the perfect place for dining alfresco. Upstairs, two secondary bedrooms—with built-in window seats—share a full hall bath, while the master suite features a walk-in closet and a private bath.

Width 60'-0"
Depth 54'-0"

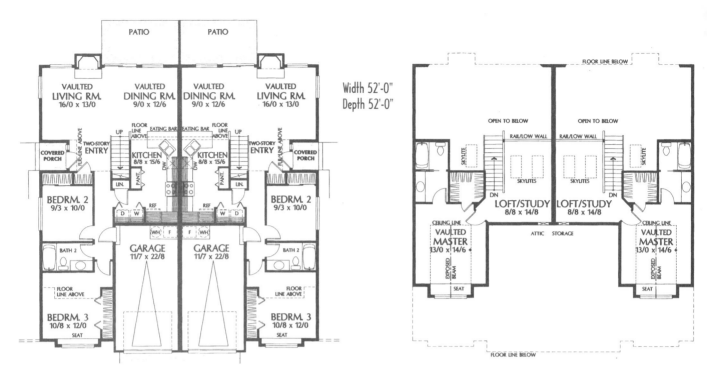

Design C524

First Floor: 1,022 square feet
Second Floor: 509 square feet
Total: 1,531 square feet per unit

Design by
Piercy & Barclay
Designers, Inc.

◆ Fine details combine with smart planning on this two-story duplex. On each unit a covered walkway leads to the covered porch entryway where a two-story foyer waits to greet you. A vaulted living room features a fireplace and windows and flows into the dining area with ease, providing the perfect place for entertaining. An efficient kitchen offers a pantry and an eating bar, with a washer/dryer closet nearby for extra convenience. Two bedrooms and a full bath complete this level. Located upstairs for privacy, the master suite features a vaulted ceiling, a walk-in closet and a private bath. A loft/study area is flooded with natural light from skylights, and finishes off this level.

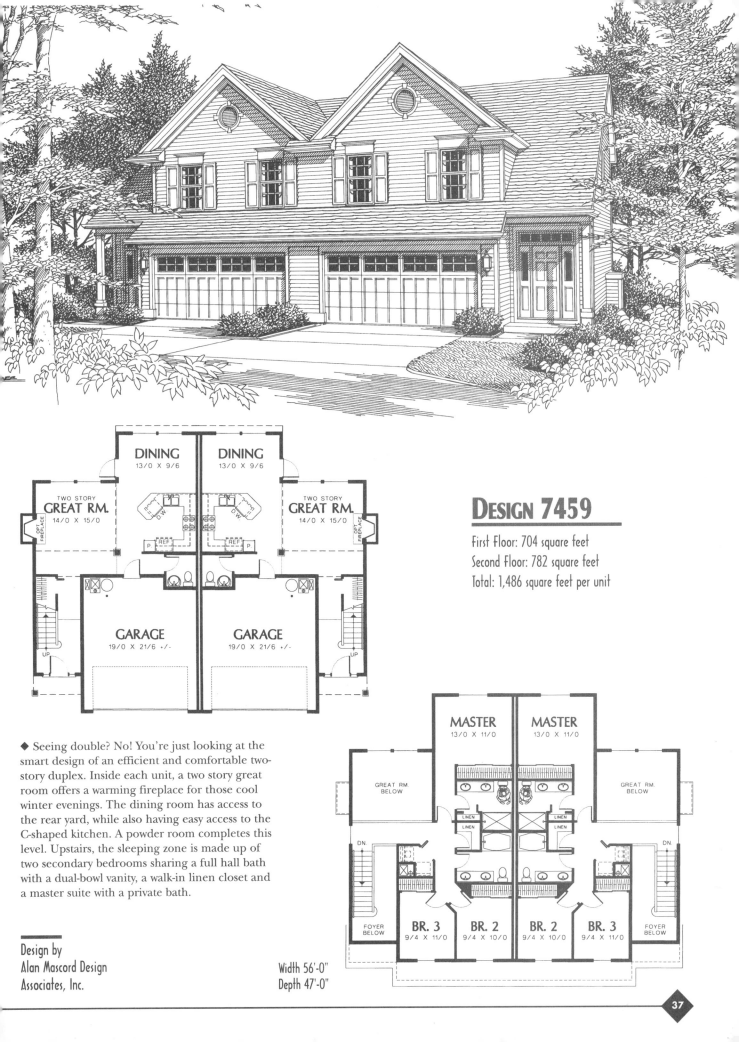

DESIGN 7459

First Floor: 704 square feet
Second Floor: 782 square feet
Total: 1,486 square feet per unit

◆ Seeing double? No! You're just looking at the smart design of an efficient and comfortable two-story duplex. Inside each unit, a two story great room offers a warming fireplace for those cool winter evenings. The dining room has access to the rear yard, while also having easy access to the C-shaped kitchen. A powder room completes this level. Upstairs, the sleeping zone is made up of two secondary bedrooms sharing a full hall bath with a dual-bowl vanity, a walk-in linen closet and a master suite with a private bath.

Design by
Alan Mascord Design
Associates, Inc.

Width 56'-0"
Depth 47'-0"

DESIGN C528

First Floor: 1,137/1,138 square feet
Second Floor: 773/793 square feet
Total: 1,910/1,931 square feet

◆ When Mike's first book sold, he decided to quit his job as a senior graphic designer and work out of his home. His wife, Anita, felt confident he'd do well, but suggested they move out of their apartment and into a house for more peace and quiet. After looking at a number of home plans, they were less sure of being able to pay all the bills that they knew they would be facing. When a good friend suggested building a duplex and renting out the second unit, Anita was all for it. Mike took a bit more convincing, but after talking with a few developers, he realized what a sound investment it would be, with the added advantage of being able to pick his own neighbors. They found a large corner lot and chose a set of fine stock plans from which to build. Their unit consisted of a sunken family room with a fireplace, and a sunken living room, both rooms with vaulted ceilings. The upstairs had three bedrooms—including the master suite—one of which could be used as Mike's office. And with a formal dining room as well as a casual nook, entertaining friends and family would be no trouble at all.

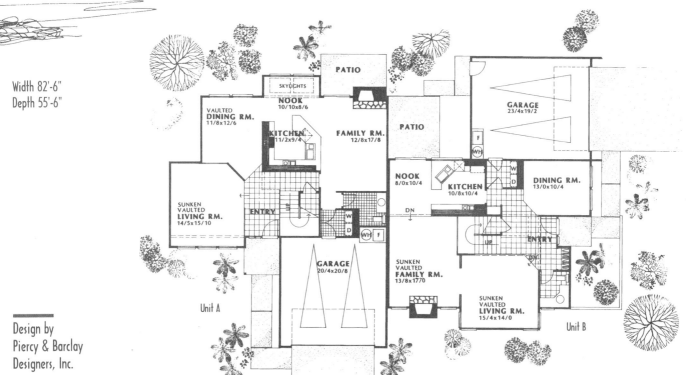

Width 82'-6"
Depth 55'-6"

Design by
Piercy & Barclay
Designers, Inc.

Design C516

First Floor: 884/924 square feet
Second Floor: 342 square feet
Total: 1,226/1,266 square feet

◆ Due to its design for a corner lot, this fine duplex looks more like a single family home. With a Northwest contemporary look, this duplex will look good in any neighborhood. Inside, a sunken living room with a stone hearth is found in both units, along with many other amenities. These include a dining room with sliding glass doors to the rear patio and easy access to the U-shaped kitchen, a secondary bedroom on the first floor and the master bedroom suite on the second floor. Here, a large closet makes up the dressing area and a private bath is ready to pamper.

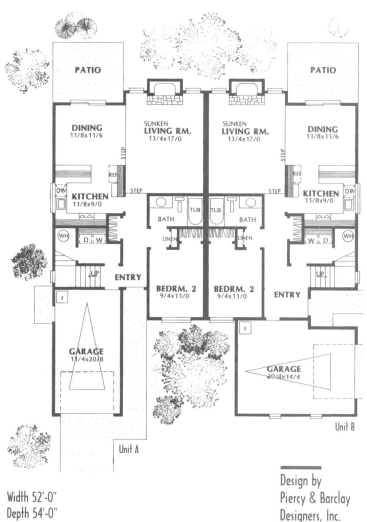

Width 52'-0"
Depth 54'-0"

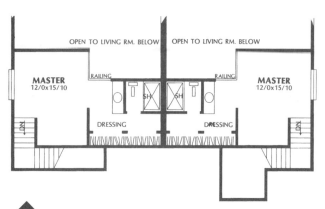

Design by
Piercy & Barclay
Designers, Inc.

Design C515

First Floor: 904 square feet
Second Floor: 360 square feet
Total: 1,264 square feet per unit

◆ Gables and angled siding combine to give this duplex plenty of curb appeal. Covered walkways lead to the entry, which then leads to a secondary bedroom on the left and back to the sunken living room. An overlook from the second-floor master bedroom suite looks into the living room and takes advantage of the warming fireplace. The U-shaped kitchen features plenty of counter and cabinet space and offers a pass-through to the dining room. Here, sliding glass doors open to a patio, providing a welcoming place for dining alfresco.

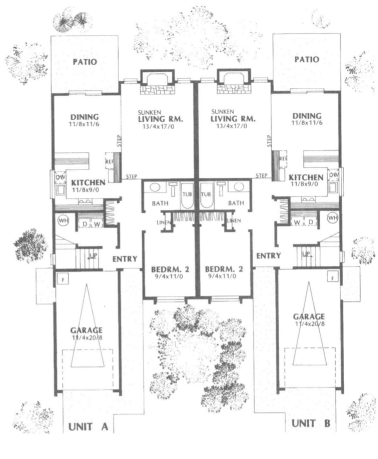

Width 52'-0"
Depth 54'-0"

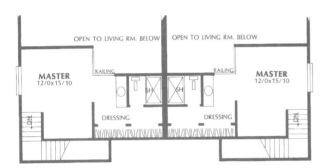

Design by
Piercy & Barclay
Designers, Inc.

Design C526

First Floor: 1,038/1,036 square feet
Second Floor: 399/571 square feet
Total: 1,437/1,607 square feet

◆ All this under one roof! This fine duplex will be perfect for any family—with young children or growing teenagers. Both units have vaulted living rooms with fireplaces and access to a rear patio. The kitchens are quite efficient, with plenty of counter and cabinet space as well as a nearby washer and dryer. In unit A, the two secondary bedrooms (or make one a study) are at opposite ends of the home from each other, while in unit B they are right next to each other. The upstairs in each unit is dedicated solely to the master suite. Here, a walk-in closet and a private bath is standard for both units.

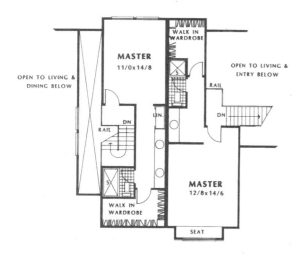

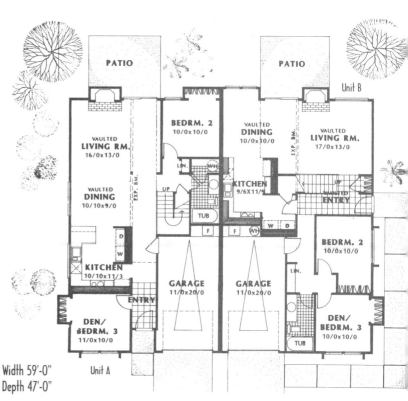

Design by
Piercy & Barclay
Designers, Inc.

Width 59'-0"
Depth 47'-0"

Design C518

First Floor: 963 square feet
Second Floor: 383 square feet
Total: 1,346 square feet per unit

◆ A covered walkway leads to an open patio and a tiled entrance for both of these mirror-image units. Inside, a vaulted morning room has access to the patio via sliding glass doors and offers easy access to the angled kitchen. The vaulted ceilings continue into the dining room and the spacious great room. Here, a stone-hearth fireplace waits to warm cool fall evenings, and there is access to the rear patio through the dining room. Located on the main floor for privacy, the master suite is complete with a walk-in closet and a private bath. Upstairs, two bedrooms—one with a window seat—share a full hall bath and a linen closet.

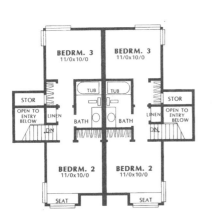

Width 68'-0"
Depth 48'-0"

Design by
Piercy & Barclay
Designers, Inc.

DESIGN C521

First Floor: 1,043 square feet
Second Floor: 464 square feet
Total: 1,507 square feet per unit

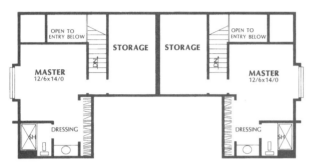

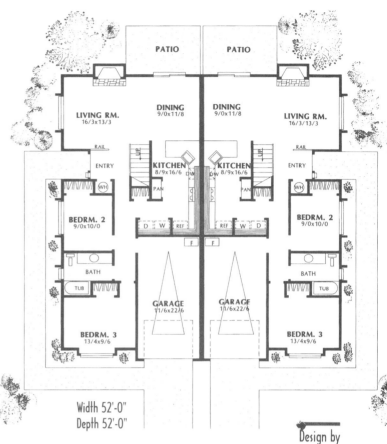

Width 52'-0"
Depth 52'-0"

◆ Mirror images of each other, these units combine to make a highly inviting duplex. Inside the foyer, a spacious living room opens to one side, enhanced by a fireplace, and flows into the dining area, perfect for easy entertaining. The kitchen offers tons of counter space, a pantry and a nearby washer and dryer. Two secondary bedrooms share a full bath and complete the first floor. Upstairs, the master suite reigns supreme, with a large dressing area and a private bath. Note the large storage room on this level.

Design by
Piercy & Barclay
Designers, Inc.

Design C520

First Floor: 760 square feet
Second Floor: 720 square feet
Total: 1,480 square feet per unit

◆ The number two is highly evident throughout this fine duplex: two units, two-car garage, two secondary bedrooms—but only one layout. From the vaulted entry one enters the vaulted great room, where a fireplace waits to warm cool evenings. The efficient kitchen has plenty of counter and cabinet space, as well as a peninsula with a sink and dishwasher. A full bath is just across the entry hall, completing this level. The sleeping zone is upstairs and consists of two secondary bedrooms and a master suite with a walk-in closet and a private lavatory. All three bedrooms share a full bath.

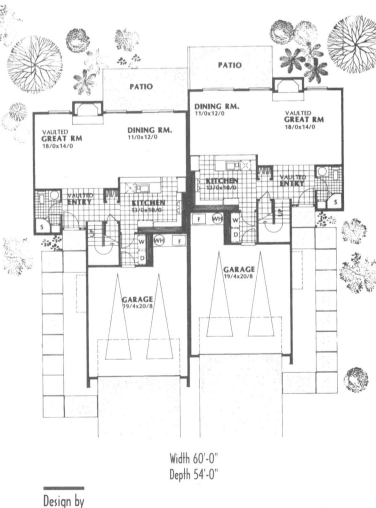

Width 60'-0"
Depth 54'-0"

Design by
Piercy & Barclay
Designers, Inc.

45

DESIGN C522

First Floor: 750 square feet
Second Floor: 766 square feet
Total: 1,516 square feet per unit

◆ As alike as two peas in a pod, this fine duplex presents two wonderful units to call home. Enter through a walled breakfast patio which is accessed from the entry and the vaulted morning room. Inside, the great room features a warming fireplace and rear yard access. The L-shaped kitchen offers an angled work island and a pantry. A utility/bathroom and a linen closet complete this floor. Upstairs, the master bedroom suite is designed to pamper, with a walk-in closet, a dressing area and a private bath. A huge den—or make it a bedroom—has views down into the entry and morning room. A secondary bedroom has access to a full hall bath.

Design by
Piercy & Barclay
Designers, Inc.

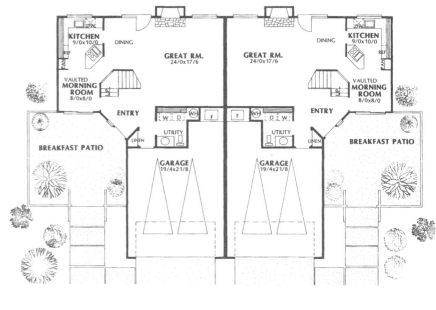

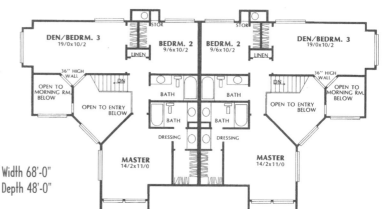

Width 68'-0"
Depth 48'-0"

Design 7453

First Floor: 620 square feet
Second Floor: 832 square feet
Total: 1,452 square feet per unit

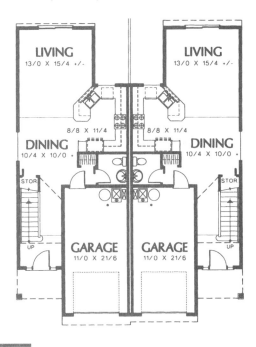

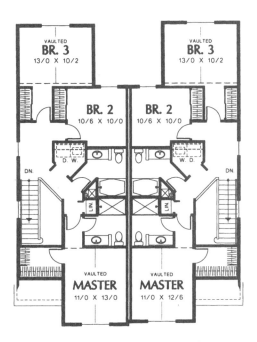

Width 40'-0"
Depth 52'-6"

Design by
Alan Mascord Design Associates, Inc.

◆ Two families fit nicely in this practical duplex plan in which each side is 20 feet wide and a mirror image of the other. Enter the home through the foyer or the garage to the open dining room/living room combination. The angled counter of the adjacent kitchen overlooks the living room, which has sliding doors to the outside. A powder room and two closets are also on the first floor. Upstairs, two family bedrooms share a hall bath, while the vaulted master suite includes a private bath and a walk-in closet. A linen closet and laundry facilities are located on this floor

Design C529

First Floor: 754 square feet
Second Floor: 405 square feet
Total: 1,159 square feet per unit

Design by
Piercy & Barclay
Designers, Inc.

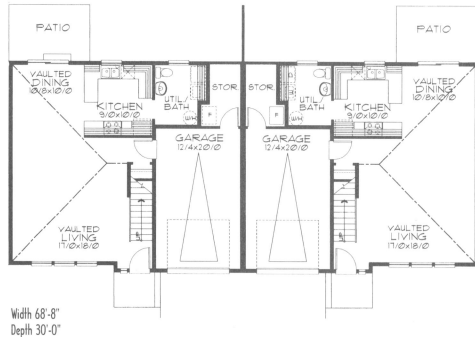

Width 68'-8"
Depth 30'-0"

◆ Two-stories, two units, twice the pleasure. The entry opens directly into the spacious, vaulted living room, which shares space with the vaulted dining room. The U-shaped kitchen easily serves this room, and offers plenty of counter and cabinet space. Upstairs, two bedrooms—one with a walk-in closet—share a full hall bath and access to a linen closet. Note the large storage room in the one-car garage.

DESIGN C527

First Floor: 940 square feet
Second Floor: 827 square feet
Total: 1,767 square feet per unit

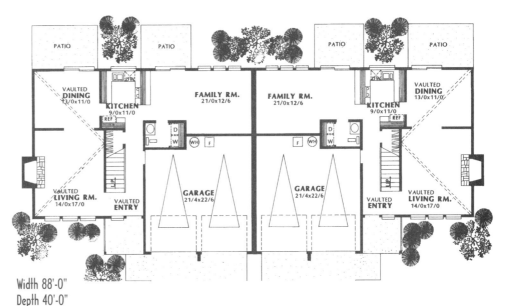

Design by
Piercy & Barclay
Designers, Inc.

Width 88'-0"
Depth 40'-0"

◆ Perfect for a growing family, this attractive duplex would look good in any neighborhood. The vaulted foyer leads to a vaulted living room, warmed by a welcoming fireplace, and down a hall to the spacious family room. Here, a wall of windows lets in plenty of natural light, while sliding glass doors provide access to a rear patio. The U-shaped kitchen easily serves this room as well as the vaulted dining room—which also offers access to a patio. Upstairs, two secondary bedrooms share a hall bath and a linen closet, while the master bedroom suite is complete with a walk-in closet, a dressing area and a private bath. The two-car garage will easily shelter the family fleet and features storage space.

FRONT VIEW
BASIC VERSION

FRONT VIEW
ENHANCED VERSION

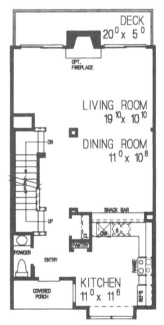

Design by
Home Planners

Width 21'-0"
Depth 36'-0"

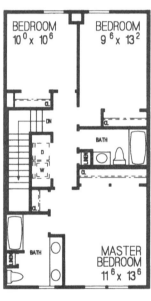

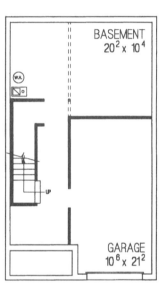

REAR VIEW
ENHANCED VERSION

Design 3737

First Floor: 685 square feet
Second Floor: 760 square feet
Total: 1,445 square feet

◆ Perfect on a narrow, sloped lot, or joined to two or more similar homes to form a set of townhouses, this efficient plan is sure to please. There is even a choice of elevations—a simpler, basic version and the enhanced version with gables. The first floor features an efficient kitchen with a snack bar, a powder room and a combined living room/dining room with an optional fireplace. Upstairs are a private master suite, two bedrooms sharing a bath and a convenient laundry area.

FRONT VIEW
BASIC VERSION

FRONT VIEW
ENHANCED VERSION

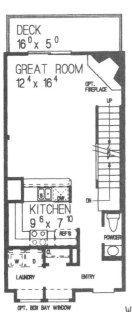

Width 17'-0"
Depth 34'-0"

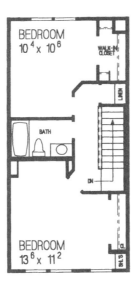

REAR VIEW
ENHANCED VERSION

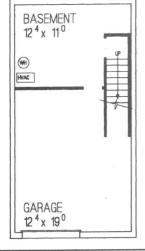

Design 3735

First Floor: 523 square feet
Second Floor: 544 square feet
Total: 1,067 square feet

Design by
Home Planners

◆ Perfect on a narrow, front-sloped lot, or joined to two or more similar dwellings to form a set of townhouses, this efficient plan is sure to please. There is even a choice of elevations—a simpler, basic version and the enhanced version with gables and a box-bay window. The first floor features an efficient U-shaped kitchen with a snack bar, a powder room and a great room with a optional corner fireplace and rear deck. Upstairs are two bedrooms—one with a walk-in closet and one with built-in shelves—sharing a bath. The garage is tucked up under the first floor.

Design 3734

First Floor: 523 square feet
Second Floor: 544 square feet
Total: 1,067 square feet

◆ Perfect on a narrow, rear-sloped lot—or join it to two or more similar homes to form a set of townhouses—this efficient plan is perfect for a first time builder. There is even a choice of elevations—a simpler, basic version and the enhanced version with gables and a box-bay window—both have attractive shutters. The first floor features an efficient U-shaped kitchen with a snack bar, a powder room and a great room with a optional corner fireplace and rear deck. Note the coat closet and laundry room at the front in the box bay. Upstairs are two bedrooms—one with a walk-in closet and one with built-in shelves—sharing a bath. The garage is tucked under the first floor.

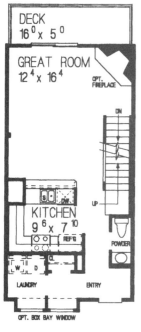

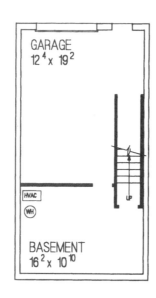

Width 17'-0"
Depth 34'-0"

Design by
Home Planners

**FRONT VIEW
BASIC VERSION**

**FRONT VIEW
ENHANCED VERSION**

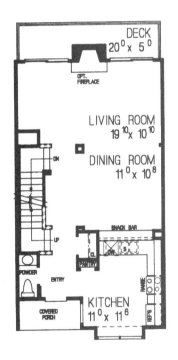

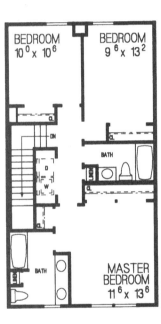

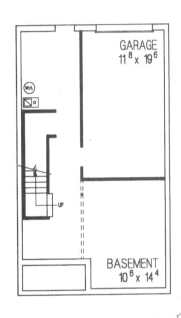

Width 21'-0"
Depth 36'-0"

Design by
Home Planners

**REAR VIEW
ENHANCED VERSION**

Design 3736

First Floor: 685 square feet
Second Floor: 760 square feet
Total: 1,445 square feet

◆ Perfect on a narrow, sloped lot, or joined to two or more dwellings to form a set of townhouses, this efficient plan is sure to please. There is even a choice of elevations—a simpler, basic version and the enhanced version with gables. The first floor features an efficient kitchen with a snack bar and box-bay window, a powder room and a combined living room/dining room with an optional fireplace and deck. Upstairs are a private master suite, two bedrooms sharing a bath and a convenient laundry room.

Design G231

◆ A playset with a little bit of everything. The Swings: This playset is designed to use any of the shelf-style swing units available at your local supplier. The Slides: There are two slides, one regular, the other an enclosed spiral slide to provide added thrills. The Ramp: The ramp is designed for kids who like to climb back up the slide. Now they can climb up the ramp and slide down the slide on the other side. For small children, you can add a knotted rope to help them up. The Eagle's Nest: The climb to the Eagle's Nest will provide your kids with exercise for their muscles and their imagination. Young children will love to switch from one part of this playset to another over and over again.

Design by
Home Planners

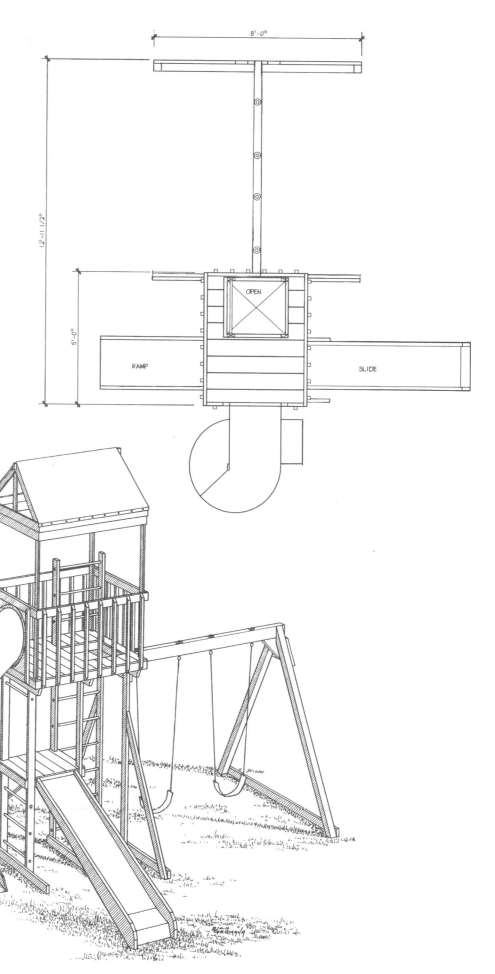

Design G232

◆ Your kids will love going up the ladder, across the swinging bridge, out on the platform, and down the firefighter's pole! The highlight of this delightful playset is the swinging bridge. It is available ready-made in a variety of styles or you can make it yourself. Either way, be sure to check that the handrail is high enough to prevent small children from toppling over the top or falling through the sides.

Designed for kids five and older, this playset includes a ladder inset at an angle to help developmental coordination. Both shelf-style swings and a popular tire swing are provided for variety. Hardware for the swings is available from your local suppliers. For larger tire swings, simply extend the support beam to accept a larger swing area. This playset is designed to sit on the ground; however, the firefighter's pole should be sunk into the ground 6" to 8" to give it additional stability.

Design by
Home Planners

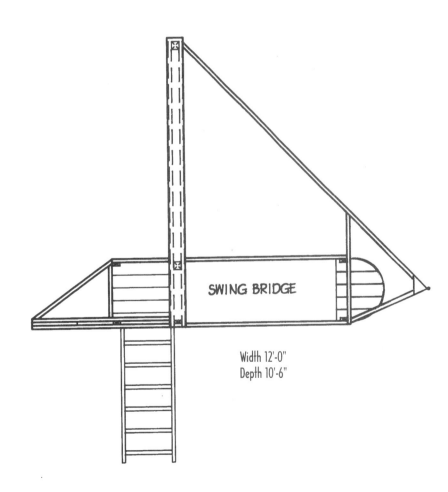

Width 12'-0"
Depth 10'-6"

When You're Ready To Order...

Let Us Show You Our Home Blueprint Package.

Building a home? Planning a home? Our Blueprint Package has nearly everything you need to get the job done right, whether you're working on your own or with help from an architect, designer, builder or subcontractors. Each Blueprint Package is the result of many hours of work by licensed architects or professional designers.

QUALITY
Hundreds of hours of painstaking effort have gone into the development of your blueprint set. Each home has been quality-checked by professionals to insure accuracy and buildability.

VALUE
Because we sell in volume, you can buy professional-quality blueprints at a fraction of their development cost. With our plans, your dream home design costs only a few hundred dollars, not the thousands of dollars that custom architects charge.

SERVICE
Once you've chosen your favorite home plan, you'll receive fast, efficient service whether you choose to mail or fax your order to us or call us toll free at 1-800-521-6797. For customer service, call toll free 1-888-690-1116.

SATISFACTION
Over 50 years of service to satisfied home plan buyers provide us unparalleled experience and knowledge in producing quality blueprints. What this means to you is satisfaction with our product and performance.

ORDER TOLL FREE 1-800-521-6797
After you've looked over our Blueprint Package and Important Extras on the following pages, simply mail the order form on page 61 or call toll free on our Blueprint Hotline: 1-800-521-6797. We're ready and eager to serve you. For customer service, call toll free 1-888-690-1116.

Each set of blueprints is an interrelated collection of detail sheets which includes components such as floor plans, interior and exterior elevations, dimensions, cross-sections, diagrams and notations. These sheets show exactly how your house is to be built.

Among the sheets included may be:

Frontal Sheet
This artist's sketch of the exterior of the house gives you an idea of how the house will look when built and landscaped. Large ink-line floor plans show all levels of the house and provide an overview of your new home's livability, as well as a handy reference for deciding on furniture placement.

Foundation Plan
This sheet shows the foundation layout includ-

SAMPLE PACKAGE

ing support walls, excavated and unexcavated areas, if any, and foundation notes. If slab construction rather than basement, the plan shows footings and details for a monolithic slab. This page, or another in the set, may include a sample plot plan for locating your house on a building site.

Detailed Floor Plans
These plans show the layout of each floor of the house. Rooms and interior spaces are carefully dimensioned and keys are given for cross-section details provided later in the plans. The positions of electrical outlets and switches are shown.

House Cross-Sections
Large-scale views show sections or cut-aways of the foundation, interior walls, exterior walls, floors, stairways and roof details. Additional cross-sections may show important changes in floor, ceiling or roof heights or the relationship of one level to another. Extremely valuable for construction, these sections show exactly how the various parts of the house fit together.

Interior Elevations
Many of our drawings show the design and placement of kitchen and bathroom cabinets, laundry areas, fireplaces, bookcases and other built-ins. Little "extras," such as mantelpiece and wainscoting drawings, plus moulding sections, provide details that give your home that custom touch.

Exterior Elevations
These drawings show the front, rear and sides of your house and give necessary notes on exterior materials and finishes. Particular attention is given to cornice detail, brick and stone accents or other finish items that make your home unique.

Price Schedule & Plans Index

House Blueprint Price Schedule
(Prices guaranteed through December 31, 1999)

Tier	1-set Study Package	4-set Building Package	8-set Building Package	1-set Reproducible Sepias	Home Customizer® Package
A	$390	$435	$495	$595	$645
B	$430	$475	$535	$655	$705
C	$470	$515	$575	$715	$765
D	$510	$555	$615	$775	$825
E	$630	$675	$735	$835	$885
F	$730	$775	$835	$935	$985
G	$830	$875	$935	$1035	$1085

Prices for 4- or 8-set Building Packages honored only at time of original order.
Additional Identical Blueprints in same order .... $50 per set
Reverse Blueprints (mirror image) .... $50 per set
Specification Outlines .... $10 each
Materials Lists (available only for those designers listed below):

- ✱ Alan Mascord Designs $50
- ❖ Select Home Designs $50

Materials Lists for "E-F" price plans are an additional $10.

Deck Plans Price Schedule

CUSTOM DECK PLANS

Price Group	Q	R	S
1 Set Custom Plans	$25	$30	$35

Additional identical sets $10 each
Reverse sets (mirror image) $10 each

STANDARD DECK DETAILS
1 Set Generic Construction Details .... $14.95 each

COMPLETE DECK BUILDING PACKAGE

Price Group	Q	R	S
1 Set Custom Plans, plus 1 Set Standard Deck Details $35		$40	$45

Landscape Plans Price Schedule

Price Group	X	Y	Z
1 set	$35	$45	$55
3 sets	$50	$60	$70
6 sets	$65	$75	$85

Additional Identical Sets .... $10 each
Reverse Sets (mirror image) .... $10 each

Index

To use the Index below, refer to the design number listed in numerical order (a helpful page reference is also given). Note the price index letter and refer to the House Blueprint Price Schedule above for the cost of one, four or eight sets of blueprints or the cost of a reproducible sepia. Additional prices are shown for identical and reverse blueprint sets, as well as a very useful Materials List for some of the plans. Also note in the Index below those plans that have matching or complementary Deck Plans or Landscape Plans. Refer to the schedules above for prices of these plans. All Home Planners' plans can be customized with Home Planners' Home Customizer® Package. These plans are indicated below with this symbol: ⌂. See page 61 for information.

To Order: Fill in and send the order form on page 61—or call toll free 1-800-521-6797 or 520-297-8200.

DESIGN	PRICE	PAGE	CUSTOMIZABLE	QUOTE ONE®	DECK	DECK PRICE	LANDSCAPE	LANDSCAPE PRICE	REGIONS
3734	C	52	⌂						
3735	C	51	⌂						
3736	C	53	⌂						
3737	C	50	⌂						
7451	D	9							
7452	D	3							
✱ 7453	D	47							
7454	D	30							
✱ 7455	D	31							
7456	D	32							
7457	D	26							
✱ 7458	E	34							
7459	D	37							
7460	D	24							
C500	D	28							
C501	D	25							
C502	A	18							
C503	A	6							
C504	B	23							
C505	B	8							
C506	B	13							
C507	B	14							
C508	B	12							
C509	C	16							
C510	B	17							
C511	C	20							
C512	C	7							
C513	C	15							
C514	C	19							
C515	C	41							
C516	C	40							
C517	C	21							
C518	C	43							
C519	C	22							
C520	C	45							
C521	D	44							
C522	D	46							
C523	D	35							
C524	D	36							
C525	D	33							
C526	D	42							
C527	D	49							
C528	D	38							
C529	B	48							
G231	$20	54							
G232	$20	55							
❖ Q453	C	29							
U188	B	10							
U192	D	4							
Z047	A	5							

Additional sets for G231-G232 are $10 each.

CONSTRUCTION INFORMATION

If you want to know more about techniques—and deal more confidently with subcontractors we offer these useful sheets. Each set is an excellent tool that will add to your understanding of these technical subjects.

Plan-A-Home®

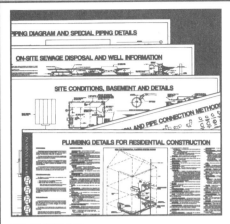

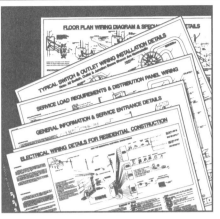

PLUMBING

The Blueprint Package includes locations for all the plumbing fixtures in your new house, including sinks, lavatories, tubs, showers, toilets, laundry trays and water heaters. However, if you want to know more about the complete plumbing system, these 24x36-inch detail sheets will prove very useful. Prepared to meet requirements of the National Plumbing Code, these six fact-filled sheets give general information on pipe schedules, fittings, sump-pump details, water-softener hookups, septic system details and much more. Color-coded sheets include a glossary of terms.

ELECTRICAL

The locations for every electrical switch, plug and outlet are shown in your Blueprint Package. However, these Electrical Details go further to take the mystery out of household electrical systems. Prepared to meet requirements of the National Electrical Code, these comprehensive 24x36-inch drawings come packed with helpful information, including wire sizing, switch-installation schematics, cable-routing details, appliance wattage, door-bell hook-ups, typical service panel circuitry and much more. Six sheets are bound together and color-coded for easy reference. A glossary of terms is also included.

Plan-A-Home® is an easy-to-use tool that helps you design a new home, arrange furniture in a new or existing home, or plan a remodeling project. Each package contains:

- **More than 700 reusable peel-off planning symbols** on a self-stick vinyl sheet, including walls, windows, doors, all types of furniture, kitchen components, bath fixtures and many more.

- **A reusable, transparent, 1/4-inch scale planning grid** that matches the scale of actual working drawings (1/4-inch equals 1 foot). This grid provides the basis for house layouts of up to 140x92 feet.

- **Tracing paper** and a protective sheet for copying or transferring your completed plan.

- **A felt-tip pen,** with water-soluble ink that wipes away quickly.

Plan-A-Home® lets you lay out areas as large as a 7,500 square foot, six-bedroom, seven-bath house.

CONSTRUCTION

The Blueprint Package contains everything an experienced builder needs to construct a particular house. However, it doesn't show all the ways that houses can be built, nor does it explain alternate construction methods. To help you understand how your house will be built—and offer additional techniques—this set of drawings depicts the materials and methods used to build foundations, fireplaces, walls, floors and roofs. Where appropriate, the drawings show acceptable alternatives. These six sheets will answer questions for the advanced do-it-yourselfer or home planner.

MECHANICAL

This package contains fundamental principles and useful data that will help you make informed decisions and communicate with subcontractors about heating and cooling systems. The 24x36-inch drawings contain instructions and samples that allow you to make simple load calculations and preliminary sizing and costing analysis. Covered are today's most commonly used systems from heat pumps to solar fuel systems. The package is packed full of illustrations and diagrams to help you visualize components and how they relate to one another.

To Order, Call Toll Free 1-800-521-6797

To add these important extras to your Blueprint Package, simply indicate your choices on the order form on page 61 or call us Toll Free 1-800-521-6797 and we'll tell you more about these exciting products.
For customer service, call toll free 1-888-690-1116.

59

Before You Order...

Before filling out the coupon at right or calling us on our Toll-Free Blueprint Hotline, you may want to learn more about our services and products. Here's some information you will find helpful.

Quick Turnaround
We process and ship every blueprint order from our office within two business days. Because of this quick turnaround, we won't send a formal notice acknowledging receipt of your order.

Our Exchange Policy
Since blueprints are printed in response to your order, we cannot honor requests for refunds. However, we will exchange your entire first order for an equal number of blueprints at a price of $50 for the first set and $10 for each additional set; $70 total exchange fee for 4 sets; $100 total exchange fee for 8 sets ... *plus* the difference in cost if exchanging for a design in a higher price bracket or *less* the difference in cost if exchanging for a design in lower price bracket. One exchange is allowed within a year of purchase date. **(Sepias are not exchangeable.)** All sets from the first order must be returned before the exchange can take place. Please add $18 for postage and handling via Regular Service; $30 via Priority Service; $40 via Express Service.

About Reverse Blueprints
If you want to build in reverse of the plan as shown, we will include an extra set of reverse blueprints (mirror image) for an additional fee of $50. Although lettering and dimensions will appear backward, reverses will be a useful aid if you decide to flop the plan.

Revising, Modifying and Customizing Plans
The wide variety of designs available in this publication allows you to select ideas and concepts for a home to fit your building site and match your family's needs, wants and budget. Like many homeowners who buy these plans, you and your builder, architect or engineer may want to make changes to them. Some minor changes may be made by your builder, but we recommend that most changes be made by a licensed architect or engineer. If you need to make alterations to a design that is customizable, you need only order our Home Customizer® Package to get you started. As set forth below, we cannot assume any responsibility for blueprints which have been changed, whether by you, your builder or by professionals selected by you or referred to you by us, because such individuals are outside our supervision and control.

Architectural and Engineering Seals
Some cities and states are now requiring that a licensed architect or engineer review and "seal" a blueprint, or officially approve it, prior to construction due to concerns over energy costs, safety and other factors. Prior to application for a building permit or the start of actual construction, we strongly advise that you consult your local building official who can tell you if such a review is required.

About the Designers
The architects and designers whose work appears in this publication are among America's leading residential designers. Each plan was designed to meet the requirements of a nationally recognized model building code in effect at the time and place the plan was drawn. Because national building codes change from time to time, plans may not comply with any such code at the time they are sold to a customer. In addition, building officials may not accept these plans as final construction documents of record as the plans may need to be modified and additional drawings and details added to suit local conditions and requirements. We strongly advise that purchasers consult a licensed architect or engineer, and their local building official, before starting any construction related to these plans.

Local Building Codes and Zoning Requirements
At the time of creation, our plans are drawn to specifications published by the Building Officials and Code Administrators (BOCA) International, Inc.; the Southern Building Code Congress (SBCCI) International, Inc.; the International Conference of Building Officials; or the Council of American Building Officials (CABO). Our plans are designed to meet or exceed national building standards. Because of the great differences in geography and climate throughout the United States and Canada, each state, county and municipality has its own building codes, zone requirements, ordinances and building regulations. Your plan may need to be modified to comply with local requirements regarding snow loads, energy codes, soil and seismic conditions and a wide range of other matters. In addition, you may need to obtain permits or inspections from local governments before and in the course of construction. Prior to using blueprints ordered from us, we strongly advise that you consult a licensed architect or engineer—and speak with your local building official—before applying for any permit or beginning construction. We authorize the use of our blueprints on the express condition that you strictly comply with all local building codes, zoning requirements and other applicable laws, regulations, ordinances and requirements. **Notice:** Plans for homes to be built in Nevada must be re-drawn by a Nevada-registered professional. Consult your building official for more information on this subject.

Foundation and Exterior Wall Changes
Most of our plans are drawn with either a full or partial basement foundation. Depending on your specific climate or regional building practices, you may wish to change this basement to a slab or crawlspace. Most professional contractors and builders can easily adapt your plans to alternate foundation types. Likewise, most can easily change 2x4 wall construction to 2x6, or vice versa.

Disclaimer
We and the designers we work with have put substantial care and effort into the creation of our blueprints. However, because we cannot provide on-site consultation, supervision and control over actual construction, and because of the great variance in local building requirements, building practices and soil, seismic, weather and other conditions, WE CANNOT MAKE ANY WARRANTY, EXPRESS OR IMPLIED, WITH RESPECT TO THE CONTENT OR USE OF OUR BLUEPRINTS, INCLUDING BUT NOT LIMITED TO ANY WARRANTY OF MERCHANTABILITY OR OF FITNESS FOR A PARTICULAR PURPOSE.

Terms and Conditions
These designs are protected under the terms of United States Copyright Law and may not be copied or reproduced in any way, by any means, unless you have purchased Sepias or Reproducibles which clearly indicate your right to copy or reproduce. We authorize the use of your chosen design as an aid in the construction of one single family home only. You may not use this design to build a second or multiple dwellings without purchasing another blueprint or blueprints or paying additional design fees.

How Many Blueprints Do You Need?
A single set of blueprints is sufficient to study a home in greater detail. However, if you are planning to obtain cost estimates from a contractor or subcontractors—or if you are planning to build immediately—you will need more sets. Because additional sets are cheaper when ordered in quantity with the original order, make sure you order enough blueprints to satisfy all requirements. The following checklist will help you determine how many you need:

____ Owner

____ Builder (generally requires at least three sets; one as a legal document, one to use during inspections, and at least one to give to subcontractors)

____ Local Building Department (often requires two sets)

____ Mortgage Lender (usually one set for a conventional loan; three sets for FHA or VA loans)

____ TOTAL NUMBER OF SETS

Have You Seen Our Newest Designs?

Home Planners is one of the country's most active home design firms, creating nearly 100 new plans each year. At least 50 of our latest creations are featured in each edition of our New Design Portfolio. You may have received a copy with your latest purchase by mail. If not, or if you purchased this book from a local retailer, just return the coupon below for your FREE copy. Make sure you consider the very latest of what Home Planners has to offer.

Yes! Please send my FREE copy of your latest New Design Portfolio.

Offer good to U.S. shipping address only.

Name _____

Address _____

City_____ State_____ Zip _____

Order Form Key
| MFB82-1 |

HOME PLANNERS, LLC
Wholly owned by Hanley-Wood, Inc.
3275 WEST INA ROAD, SUITE 110
TUCSON, ARIZONA 85741

Toll Free 1-800-521-6797
Regular Office Hours:
8:00 a.m. to 8:00 p.m. Eastern Time, Monday through Friday
Our staff will gladly answer any questions during regular office hours. Our answering service can place orders after hours or on weekends.

If we receive your order by 4:00 p.m. Eastern Time, Monday through Friday, we'll process it and ship within two business days. When ordering by phone, please have your charge card ready. We'll also ask you for the Order Form Key Number at the bottom of the coupon.

By FAX: Copy the Order Form on the next page and send it on our FAX line: 1-800-224-6699 or 1-520-544-3086.

Canadian Customers
Order Toll-Free 1-800-561-4169

For faster service and plans that are modified for building in Canada, customers may now call in orders directly to our Canadian supplier of plans and charge the purchase to a charge card. Or, you may complete the order form at right, adding 40% to all prices and mail in Canadian funds to:

The Plan Centre 60 Baffin Place
Unit 5
Waterloo, Ontario N2V 1Z7

OR: Copy the Order Form and send it via our Canadian FAX line: 1-800-719-3291.

SPECIFICATION OUTLINE

This valuable 16-page document is critical to building your house correctly. Designed to be filled in by you or your builder, this book lists 166 stages or items crucial to the building process. It provides a comprehensive review of the construction process and helps in making choices of materials. When combined with the blueprints, a signed contract, and a schedule, it becomes a legal document and record for the building of your home.

MATERIALS LIST

For many of the designs in our portfolio, we offer a customized materials take-off that is invaluable in planning and estimating the cost of your new home. This Materials List outlines the quantity, type and size of materials needed to build your house (with the exception of mechanical system items). Included are framing lumber, windows and doors, kitchen and bath cabinetry, rough and finish hardware, and much more. This handy list helps you or your builder cost out materials and serves as a reference sheet when you're compiling bids. A Materials List cannot be ordered before blueprints are ordered. (Note: Because of the diversity of local building codes, our Materials List does not include mechanical materials.)

 ORDER TOLL FREE!
1-800-521-6797 or 520-297-8200
www.homeplanners.com

BLUEPRINTS ARE NOT RETURNABLE

For Customer Service,
call toll free 1-888-690-1116.

ORDER FORM

 HOME PLANNERS, LLC
Wholly owned by Hanley-Wood, Inc.
3275 WEST INA ROAD, SUITE 110
TUCSON, ARIZONA 85741

THE BASIC BLUEPRINT PACKAGE
Rush me the following (please refer to the Plans Index and Price Schedule in this section):
_____ Set(s) of blueprints for plan number(s) _____. $_____
_____ Set(s) of sepias for plan number(s) _____. $_____
_____ Home Customizer® Package for plan(s)_____. $_____
_____ Additional identical blueprints in same order @ $50 per set. $_____
_____ Reverse blueprints @ $50 per set. $_____

IMPORTANT EXTRAS
Rush me the following:
_____ Materials List: $50 (Must be purchased with Blueprint set.)
$75 Design Basics. Add $10 for a Schedule E plan Materials List. $_____
_____ **Quote One**® Materials Cost Report @ $110 Schedule A-D; $120
Schedule E for plan_____ $_____
(Must be purchased with Blueprints set.)
Building location: City _____Zip Code _____
_____ Specification Outlines @ $10 each. $_____
_____ Detail Sets @ $14.95 each; any two for $22.95; any three
for $29.95; all four for $39.95 (save $19.85). $_____
❏ Plumbing ❏ Electrical ❏ Construction ❏ Mechanical
(These helpful details provide general construction
advice and are not specific to any single plan.)
_____ Plan-A-Home® @ $29.95 each. $_____

POSTAGE AND HANDLING	1-3 sets	4+ sets
Signature is required for all deliveries. **DELIVERY** (Requires street address - No P.O. Boxes)		
•Regular Service (Allow 7-10 business days delivery)	❏ $15.00	❏ $18.00
•Priority (Allow 4-5 business days delivery)	❏ $20.00	❏ $30.00
•Express (Allow 3 business days delivery)	❏ $30.00	❏ $40.00
CERTIFIED MAIL If no street address available. (Allow 7-10 days delivery)	❏ $20.00	❏ $30.00
OVERSEAS DELIVERY Note: All delivery times are from date Blueprint Package is shipped.	fax, phone or mail for quote	

POSTAGE (From box above) $_____
SUB-TOTAL $_____
SALES TAX (AZ, CA, DC, IL, MI, MN, NY & WA residents,
please add appropriate state and local sales tax.) $_____
TOTAL (Sub-total and tax) $_____

YOUR ADDRESS (please print)
Name _____
Street _____
City _____State_____Zip _____
Daytime telephone number (_____) _____

FOR CREDIT CARD ORDERS ONLY
Please fill in the information below:
Credit card number _____
Exp. Date: Month/Year _____
Check one ❏ Visa ❏ MasterCard ❏ Discover Card ❏ American Express

Signature _____

Please check appropriate box: ❏ Licensed Builder-Contractor
❏ Homeowner

ORDER TOLL FREE!
1-800-521-6797 or 520-297-8200

Order Form Key
MFB82-1

Helpful Books & Software

Home Planners wants your building experience to be as pleasant and trouble-free as possible. That's why we've expanded our library of Do-It-Yourself titles to help you along. In addition to our beautiful plans books, we've added books to guide you through specific projects as well as the construction process. In fact, these are titles that will be as useful after your dream home is built as they are right now.

ONE-STORY

1 448 designs for all lifestyles. 860 to 5,400 square feet. 384 pages $9.95

TWO-STORY

2 460 designs for one-and-a-half and two stories. 1,245 to 7,275 square feet. 384 pages $9.95

VACATION

3 345 designs for recreation, retirement and leisure. 312 pages $8.95

MULTI-LEVEL

4 214 designs for split-levels, bi-levels, multi-levels and walkouts. 224 pages $8.95

COUNTRY

5 200 country designs from classic to contemporary by 7 winning designers. 224 pages $8.95

MOVE-UP

6 200 stylish designs for today's growing families from 9 hot designers. 224 pages $8.95

NARROW-LOT

7 200 unique homes less than 60' wide from 7 designers. Up to 3,000 square feet. 224 pages $8.95

SMALL HOUSE

8 200 beautiful designs chosen for versatility and affordability. 224 pages $8.95

BUDGET-SMART

9 200 efficient plans from 7 top designers, that you can really afford to build! 224 pages $8.95

EXPANDABLES

10 200 flexible plans that expand with your needs from 7 top designers. 240 pages $8.95

ENCYCLOPEDIA

11 500 exceptional plans for all styles and budgets—the best book of its kind! 352 pages $9.95

AFFORDABLE

12 Completely revised and updated, featuring 300 designs for modest budgets. 256 pages $9.95

ENCYCLOPEDIA 2

13 500 Completely new plans. Spacious and stylish designs for every budget and taste. 352 pages $9.95

VICTORIAN

14 160 striking Victorian and Farmhouse designs from three leading designers. 192 pages $12.95

ESTATE

15 Dream big! Twenty-one designers showcase their biggest and best plans. 208 pages. $15.95

LUXURY

16 154 fine luxury plans-loaded with luscious amenities! 192 pages $14.95

COTTAGES

17 25 fresh new designs that are as warm as a tropical breeze. A blend of the best aspects of many coastal styles. 64 pages. $19.95

BEST SELLERS

18 Our 50th Anniversary book with 200 of our very best designs in full color! 224 pages $12.95

SPECIAL COLLECTION

19 70 Romantic house plans that capture the classic tradition of home design. 160 pages $17.95

COUNTRY HOUSES

20 208 Unique home plans that combine traditional style and modern livability. 224 pages $9.95

CLASSIC

21 Timeless, elegant designs that always feel like home. Gorgeous plans that are as flexible and up-to-date as their occupants. 240 pages. $9.95

CONTEMPORARY

22 The most complete and imaginative collection of contemporary designs available anywhere. 240 pages $9.95

EASY-LIVING

23 200 Efficient and sophisticated plans that are small in size, but big on livability. 224 pages $8.95

SOUTHERN

24 207 homes rich in Southern styling and comfort. 240 pages $8.95

Design Software | Outdoor Projects

SUNBELT
25 215 Designs that capture the spirit of the Southwest. 208 pages $10.95

WESTERN

26 215 designs that capture the spirit and diversity of the Western lifestyle. 208 pages $9.95

ENERGY GUIDE

27 The most comprehensive energy efficiency and conservation guide available. 280 pages $35.00

BOOK & CD ROM

28 Both the Home Planners Gold book and matching Windows™ CD ROM with 3D floorplans. $24.95

3D DESIGN SUITE

29 Home design made easy! View designs in 3D, take a virtual reality tour, add decorating details and more. $59.95

OUTDOOR

30 42 unique outdoor projects. Gazebos, strombellas, bridges, sheds, playsets and more! 96 pages $7.95

GARAGES & MORE

31 101 Multi-use garages and outdoor structures to enhance any home. 96 pages $7.95

DECKS
32 25 outstanding single-, double- and multi-level decks you can build. 112 pages $7.95

TO ORDER BOOKS BY PHONE 1-800-322-6797

Landscape Designs

| EASY CARE | FRONT & BACK | BACKYARDS | BEDS & BORDERS | BATHROOMS | KITCHENS | HOUSE CONTRACTING | WINDOWS & DOORS |

     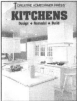 

33 41 special landscapes designed for beauty and low maintenance. 160 pages $14.95

34 The first book of do-it-yourself landscapes. 40 front, 15 backyards. 208 pages $14.95

35 40 designs focused solely on creating your own specially themed backyard oasis. 160 pages $14.95

36 Practical advice and maintenance techniques for a wide variety of yard projects. 160 pages. $14.95

37 An innovative guide to organizing, remodeling and decorating your bathroom. 96 pages $9.95

38 An imaginative guide to designing the perfect kitchen. Chock full of bright ideas to make your job easier. 176 pages $14.95

39 Everything you need to know to act as your own general contractor...and save up to 25% off building costs. 134 pages $14.95

40 Installation techniques and tips that make your project easier and more professional looking. 80 pages $7.95

| ROOFING | FRAMING | VISUAL HANDBOOK | BASIC WIRING | PATIOS & WALKS | TILE | TRIM & MOLDING |

  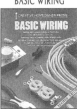  

41 Information on the latest tools, materials and techniques for roof installation or repair. 80 pages $7.95

42 For those who want to take a more-hands on approach to their dream. 319 pages $19.95

43 A plain-talk guide to the construction process; financing to final walk-through, this book covers it all. 498 pages $19.95

44 A straight forward guide to one of the most misunderstood systems in the home. 160 pages $12.95

45 Clear step-by-step instructions take you from the basic design stages to the finished project. 80 pages $7.95

46 Every kind of tile for every kind of application. Includes tips on use installation and repair. 176 pages $12.95

47 Step-by-step instructions for installing baseboards, window and door casings and more. 80 pages $7.95

Additional Books Order Form

To order your books, just check the box of the book numbered below and complete the coupon. We will process your order and ship it from our office within 48 hours. Send coupon and check (in U.S. funds).

YES! Please send me the books I've indicated:

- ☐ 1:VO $9.95
- ☐ 2:VT $9.95
- ☐ 3:VH $8.95
- ☐ 4:VS $8.95
- ☐ 5:FH $8.95
- ☐ 6:MU $8.95
- ☐ 7:NL $8.95
- ☐ 8:SM $8.95
- ☐ 9:BS $8.95
- ☐ 10:EX $8.95
- ☐ 11:EN $9.95
- ☐ 12:AF $9.95
- ☐ 13:E2 . . . . $9.95
- ☐ 14:VDH $12.95
- ☐ 15:EDH $15.95
- ☐ 16:LD2 . . . . $14.95
- ☐ 17:CTG $19.95
- ☐ 18:HPG $12.95
- ☐ 19:WEP $17.95
- ☐ 20:CN $9.95
- ☐ 21:CS $9.95
- ☐ 22:CM $9.95
- ☐ 23:EL $8.95
- ☐ 24:SH $8.95
- ☐ 25:SW $10.95
- ☐ 26:WH $9.95
- ☐ 27:RES $35.00
- ☐ 28:HPGC $24.95
- ☐ 29:PLANSUITE . . $59.95
- ☐ 30:YG $7.95
- ☐ 31:GG $7.95
- ☐ 32:DP $7.95
- ☐ 33:ECL $14.95
- ☐ 34:HL $14.95
- ☐ 35:BYL $14.95
- ☐ 36:BB $14.95
- ☐ 37:CDB $9.95
- ☐ 38:CKI $14.95
- ☐ 39:SBC $14.95
- ☐ 40:CGD $7.95
- ☐ 41:CGR $7.95
- ☐ 42:SRF $19.95
- ☐ 43:RVH $19.95
- ☐ 44:CBW $12.95
- ☐ 45:CGW $7.95
- ☐ 46:CWT $12.95
- ☐ 47:CGT $7.95

Canadian Customers
Order Toll-Free 1-800-561-4169

Additional Books Sub-Total $_____
ADD Postage and Handling $ 4.00
Sales Tax: (AZ, CA, DC, IL, MI, MN, NY & WA residents, please add appropriate state and local sales tax.) $_____
YOUR TOTAL (Sub-Total, Postage/Handling, Tax) $_____

YOUR ADDRESS (Please print)

Name _____

Street _____

City _____ State_____ Zip _____

Phone (_____) _____ — _____

YOUR PAYMENT
Check one: ☐ Check ☐ Visa ☐ MasterCard ☐ Discover Card ☐ American Express
Required credit card information:
Credit Card Number _____

Expiration Date (Month/Year) _____/_____

Signature Required _____

 Home Planners, LLC
Wholly owned by Hanley-Wood, Inc.
3275 W. Ina Road, Suite 110, Dept. BK, Tucson, AZ 85741

MFB82-1

Design 7451, page 9

OVER 3 MILLION BLUEPRINTS SOLD

"We instructed our builder to follow the plans including all of the many details which make this house so elegant…Our home is a fine example of the results one can achieve by purchasing and following the plans which you offer…Everyone who has seen it has assured us that it belongs in 'a picture book.' I truly mean it when I say that my home 'is a DREAM HOUSE.'"

S.P.
Anderson, SC

"We have had a steady stream of visitors, many of whom tell us this is the most beautiful home they've seen. Everyone is amazed at the layout and remarks on how unique it is. Our real estate attorney, who is a Chicago dweller and who deals with highly valued properties, told me this is the only suburban home he has seen that he would want to live in."

W. & P.S.
Flossmoor, IL

"Your blueprints saved us a great deal of money. I acted as the general contractor and we did a lot of the work ourselves. We probably built it for half the cost! We are thinking about more plans for another home. I purchased a competitor's book but my husband wants only your plans!"

K.M.
Grovetown, GA

"We are very happy with the product of our efforts. The neighbors and passersby appreciate what we have created. We have had many people stop by to discuss our house and kindly praise it as being the nicest house in our area of new construction. We have even had one person stop and make us an unsolicited offer to buy the house for much more than we have invested in it."

K. & L.S.
Bolingbrook, IL

"The traffic going past our house is unbelievable. On several occasions, we have heard that it is the 'prettiest house in Batavia.' Also, when meeting someone new and mentioning what street we live on, quite often we're told, 'Oh, you're the one in the yellow house with the wrap-around porch! I love it!'"

A.W.
Batavia, NY

"I have been involved in the building trades my entire life…Since building our home we have built two other homes for other families. Their plans from local professional architects were not nearly as good as yours. For that reason we are ordering additional plan books from you."

T.F.
Kingston, WA

"The blueprints we received from you were of excellent quality and provided us with exactly what we needed to get our successful home-building project underway. We appreciate your invaluable role in our home-building effort."

T.A.
Concord, TN